Causes, Preventive Measures, and Methods of Controlling

RIOTS

& DISTURBANCES

In Correctional Institutions

Acknowledgments

The American Correctional Association would like to credit the following for providing photographs for this publication. All other photos are from ACA files.

Capitol Communication Systems, Inc.: p. 55
Michael Dersin: pp. 3, 5, 15
Federal Bureau of Prisons: pp. 40, 43, 45, 46 (bottom), 56
Florida Department of Corrections: pp. 7, 17, 23, 51 (top)
Henningson, Durham & Richardson, Inc.: pp. 21, 29

New York City Department of Corrections: p. 4
Paul Potera: pp. 10, 11, 30
South Carolina Department of Corrections: pp. 16, 46 (top)
Clinton Van Zandt, FBI Training Academy: pp. vii, 44, 49

Author: James D. Henderson
Contributing Editor: Richard L. Phillips

Publications Director: Patricia L. Millard
Project Editor: Ann Dargis
Editorial Assistant: Marie G. Unger

ISBN 0-929310-23-3

Printed in the United States of America by St. Mary's Press, Washington, D.C.

Contents

Foreword

This updated and thoroughly revised edition of *Riots and Disturbances in Correctional Institutions* summarizes the available information and experience on the causes, preventive measures, and methods of controlling riots and disturbances in correctional institutions. The purpose of this publication is to enable administrators, staff, and appropriate public officials to take necessary preventive measures, to develop a comprehensive riot control plan for each institution within their charge, and in those unfortunate instances when disturbances do occur, to take appropriate steps to quell them professionally and humanely. The material in this publication has been kept relatively broad and general. Each prison is unique, and the suggested measures need to be considered in the context of each facility's specific physical design, personnel resources, inmate population, and administrative practices.

The 1981 edition of this manual opened by noting that the volatility created by the problems of prison overcrowding—inmate idleness, understaffing, severe budget constraints, and many other contemporary management issues— can create the potential for these crisis situations. Since then, the inmate population in American correctional institutions has increased by 100 percent—from 323,000 to 673,000 (Bureau of Justice Statistics 1989). Indeed, what was true in 1981 is even more true now—and no immediate end to the growth is in sight. Even though an equally unprecedented prison construction boom is under way in many states and the federal prison system, these additional beds will be far from adequate to keep pace with the anticipated inmate population growth in the next decade.

Thus, the need is far more urgent now than in 1981 for correctional administrators and subordinate personnel to be well-versed in preventing and handling riots and disturbances. More than ever, staff training, comprehensive emergency response plans, functional decision-making strategies, advance response strategies, and cooperative inter-agency agreements must be part of an agency's crisis management strategy.

In the 1981 edition of this publication, the images of recent disturbances at Attica, N.Y., and Santa Fe, N.M., were still fresh. Indeed, it is an unfortunate fact that each such incident provides a difficult and dramatic, yet valuable, learning experience for correctional professionals everywhere. And so, with this edition, another set of disturbances provides fresh lessons—the 1987 Cuban detainee disturbances in Oakdale, La., and Atlanta, Ga.[1] This was the most recent set of major prison disturbances in this country, and the references to them in this publication do not reflect any particular view with regard to the Bureau of Prisons. They are highlighted when

---

[1]The U.S. Bureau of Prisons confined about 2,500 Cuban detainees at its Oakdale and Atlanta facilities in the fall of 1987. In November of that year, the State Department, unbeknownst to the Bureau, concluded an agreement with the Cuban government that, on its surface, would have appeared to the detainees to result in their involuntary repatriation, or deportation, to Cuba. Within days of the announcement, both institutions were completely overrun by the detainees. In Oakdale, 28 employees were held hostage; in Atlanta, there were 102 staff hostages. After protracted negotiations in an atmosphere of extraordinary law enforcement presence, military reinforcements, and media interest, the sieges were concluded with the release of all hostages at both sites. No staff were killed throughout the two weeks of the disturbances, and only one inmate was killed, during the initial takeover when he was seen chasing a staff member with a knife and was shot from a tower. The negotiations for the hostages' release centered not around prison conditions, but rather the political agreement that would have led to the repatriation of the rioters. The agreement that settled the riots likewise was a non-prison accord.

they convey some important lesson for the field of corrections as a whole. They provide important additions to the body of professional knowledge we all rely on, complementing traditional wisdom in some respects, contradicting it in others.[2]

And therein, perhaps, is the central message of this publication. There are no concrete answers, no absolute responses, no incontrovertible truths that can be applied across the board in a crisis like a riot. But sound professional judgment, coupled with knowledge of the institution, its staff and inmates, and adequate resources do provide the keys to effective responses in these sobering circumstances.

---

[2]Appendix A is a list of 107 recommendations developed by an After-Action Team commissioned by the Bureau of Prisons to suggest future management action and emergency preparedness needs. These materials are included not as a blanket endorsement of the recommendations (because the Bureau itself has not adopted all of them) but as an indicator of the depth and breadth of issues that were dealt with in that set of crises. Individual agencies may find them useful for gauging their degree of preparedness for a major disturbance.

Although prisons are the primary focus of this publication, the information is relevant to jails and therefore of interest to jail administrators as well. This information is directed to corrections personnel at all levels—administrators, middle management, and line officers. It should also be of interest to legislators, other public officials, and the concerned general public—all of whom have a stake in the prevention of further violent and costly outbreaks in our correctional institutions.

Many highly qualified correctional administrators took part in the publication of the first two volumes of this manual, published in 1970 and 1981. We hope their work, extended through this revision by yet another group of fine professionals, will be valuable to correctional managers and others who deal with this important issue.

Anthony P. Travisono
Executive Director
American Correctional Association

Introduction

The prison riot as a phenomenon can be viewed in a number of ways. To a behavioral scientist, a riot might be seen as a form of communication or expression, one used after less drastic means have proved unsuccessful. To the revolutionary, a riot may be a form of social protest and a tool for radical change. To the media, it is a rare opportunity to portray real-life drama that rivals the best of fiction. To the correctional administrator, it is a challenge to authority—an insurrection that threatens the delicate balance of power in an institution and the lives of those who live and work there.

But riots and disturbances in prisons are not a new phenomenon in the United States, and recent decades have seen a continuation of these destructive, violent events. Prison violence seems to run in cycles, and the contagious nature of major prison disturbances is an ongoing concern nationwide. The first major wave occurred during 1952 and 1953, when at least 25 different institutions had to quell revolts among their inmates, with incidents that resulted in many injuries, millions of dollars of damage, and the destruction of major facilities and equipment. After a period of relative calm, a new series of riots began in Oregon in 1968 and spread across the country. The Attica riot in 1971 and the New Mexico riot at the Santa Fe Penitentiary in 1980 resulted in loss of life, great human suffering, and major property damage.

To this list, we now can add the dual uprisings of Cuban detainees in federal institutions in Oakdale, La., and Atlanta, Ga., in the fall of 1987. These disturbances were the largest and most widespread, and they involved the largest number of hostages in U.S. prison history. They confirm many of the long-held

tenets of crisis management and provide interesting counterpoints to others.

COSTLY DAMAGE

Riots and disturbances are costly. They often result in extensive property damage, frequently totaling millions of dollars. The damages resulting from the Oakdale/Atlanta episodes, for instance, totaled approximately $100 million. In these days of dwindling resources and budgets that fail to keep pace with escalating inmate population increases, replacing riot-damaged or destroyed buildings and equipment often becomes a fiscal impossibility. In contrast to the fiscal toll (which can be remedied), the damaging physical and psychological effects on staff hostages and inmates, and on their families, can neither be measured nor easily alleviated.

Although more than 90 percent of all reported prison riots have occurred since 1952, the reasons for the increased frequency and violence of such eruptions are not equally well known. Improved reporting might account for a small amount of the increase in the number of riots, but other root causes must be sought.

In recent years our society has experienced dramatic changes. Crime has continued to increase, and the public's reaction resulted in prison populations soaring to an all-time high. Drug trafficking, both in the outside world and in prison, has given a new complexion to criminals and their activity. The pervasive influence of drugs in our society has penetrated correctional institutions and created new arenas for power struggles that can jeopardize security in numerous ways. Revolutionary organizations, with

their terrorist tactics, have extended their influence inside correctional institutions and are becoming a threat to ex-inmates and their families on the outside (Kahn & Zinn 1979), as well as to correctional officials themselves. Prison gangs have formed and prison violence increased, presenting similar dangers and management concerns. These phenomena seem related in some way to the power of the media (particularly television, with its wide audience and capability of instant coverage) to effectively, if sometimes inaccurately, mold and influence public attitudes. The Oakdale/Atlanta riots provide a textbook example of real-time media coverage and its impact on the course of a riot. Taken together, these factors place contemporary correctional administrators face-to-face with formidable challenges to the order of their facilities.

This publication continues to emphasize the basics—effective recruiting and training of highly professional staff; well thought-out contingency plans that staff at all levels are familiar with; appropriate equipment and training in its use; sound communications and intelligence-gathering capabilities in the institution's day-to-day operation; and the application of proven crisis management strategies. It is intended to serve as a compendium of ideas and a professional guide to developing specific agency strategies for planning, training, and making crisis response decisions.

Causes, Preventive Measures, and
Methods of Controlling
RIOTS & DISTURBANCES
In Correctional Institutions

1

Management Concerns

A correctional institution, like any other business, industry, or government agency, must have competent, professional management if it is to be operated successfully. True, many of the underlying causes of prison disturbances can ultimately be traced to circumstances beyond the control of correctional administrators. But a significant number of the conditions and practices that precipitate disturbances can be directly attributed to management practices at the institutional level.

Within an institution, some of the symptoms of administrative practices that may precede a riot or major disturbance are: vague lines of authority and administrative responsibility; the absence of clearly defined and easily understood rules and regulations; poor communications; partiality in dealing with inmates and staff; lack of familiarity by top staff with the institution, its staff, and inmates; and indecisive action on legitimate grievances.

Staff are the critical factor in any institution, from the chief executive officer through the newest line employee. If the institution's overall personnel practices are inadequate, the quality of the operation and the order of the institution will be adversely affected. This emphasis on personnel inadequacies is fundamentally important in reviewing the causes of disturbances; studying most past disturbances reveals a critical decision, a staff miscue, or some other human error was the fulcrum around which the crisis turned.

The following sections discuss how some of the common problems in hiring, training, and retaining qualified personnel might indirectly cause disturbances. Correcting these factors does not guarantee the human element will not fail in a correctional institution. But fully addressing these areas reduces the chances of a critical staff error to a minimum.

FREQUENT MANAGEMENT TURNOVER

A common, very serious problem is the tremendous turnover in correctional management in many agencies. The Criminal Justice Institute, Inc., reported that as of August 1, 1989, the average length of service of directors of adult correctional agencies in the United States was only 3.42 years. This extreme turnover inevitably causes instability at the agency level, and that instability is inevitably felt at the institutional level as well. It appears, however, that correctional appointments are becoming more political, which suggests this kind of rapid turnover is an even more likely pattern in the future.

Those in charge of appointing correctional officials should ensure that they have a competent individual at the helm, and then protect that administrator from needless political conflict. New direction and leadership may be needed from time to time, but constant and precipitous changes are almost always detrimental to the stability of agencies and their institutions. The lack of a consistent long-range vision and correctional philosophy for the agency is an incalculable deficit to organizations that are subject to the winds and whims of politically motivated personnel changes.

FREQUENT LINE STAFF TURNOVER

The high turnover of line staff, particularly correctional officers, is another serious problem. Since in most jurisdictions correctional officer pay

is low, and stress is high, and new staff are often given the least desirable jobs and shifts, it is hardly surprising that in many institutions more than 50 percent of all new correctional officers fail to complete their first year on the job.

A functional retention program must be founded on the basis of realistic qualifications and standards. Applicants should be screened by competitive examinations, and a combined emphasis on selectivity and improved personnel benefits will assure a sound foundation for developing a well-trained, professional staff.

Recruitment activity in today's demographic environment places correctional administrators in direct competition with numerous other private- and public-sector organizations for a shrinking pool of suitable candidates. Moreover, the inability of many correctional agencies to match pay and benefits within the law enforcement community means that staff often take a correctional job as a stepping stone to a higher-paying position as a state or local police officer, or with another related agency like probation or parole. In any case, the turnover and recruitment/training costs associated with high turnover rates seriously hamper operational effectiveness in an institution.

Staff are the critical factor in any institution, from the chief executive officer through the newest line employee.

Of primary importance in obtaining qualified personnel is a well-structured program of recruiting and hiring. Staff must be recruited and hired on the basis of realistic standards of qualifications, and all prospective employees should be screened by competitive examinations. There is tremendous variation in this area. In some jurisdictions, the basic qualification level for entering correctional officers is a college background; in others, far less education may suffice. In most cases, it is difficult to insist on any directly related experience for entry-level staff, because there are few nongovernment counterparts to prison work.

In order to attract the quality personnel necessary in a correctional institution, heavy emphasis must be placed on adequate salaries and satisfactory working conditions. In addition, there should be a sound merit system for promotion, attractive employee benefits, and an adequate number of positions to ensure efficient and safe working conditions. This emphasis on selectivity and improved personnel benefits will assure a sound foundation for developing a well-trained, professional staff.

Unfortunately, in a time of increasingly stringent budget constraints in most jurisdictions, these factors are not always available. Nevertheless, as a long-range strategy, responsible administrators should initiate changes within available resources. They must adopt, as a high priority, strategies that will educate the public and their funding sources about the need for changes in areas beyond their immediate control.

Specialty recruiting is another area where responsible administrators should focus their efforts. Since correctional institutions have a high percentage of inmates representing racial and ethnic minorities, it is generally considered desirable to have a similar ethnic/racial ratio among the staff. Such staffing patterns are difficult to achieve, however, since many institutions are in rural areas where there tend to be fewer minorities. Finding and retaining minority staff are problems that need considerable attention. Recruitment of qualified teachers, doctors, nurses, and other specialists is also a continuing concern.

In an interesting program at the federal level, some law enforcement agencies (although not the Bureau of Prisons) are authorized to pay Spanish-speaking staff up to 25 percent of their salary as a bonus, when that skill is deemed important to the agency's mission. Options of this type should be explored for corrections as well.

INADEQUATE STAFF TRAINING

One important factor in reducing the potential for disturbances is having efficient personnel who can handle their responsibilities and any emergencies in a calm, confident manner. This attitude most often comes from thorough training in necessary technical and interpersonal skills. A trained employee will respond to urgent situations quickly, logically, and with a minimum of wasted effort. Appropriately designed training programs can begin to address the problems associated with lack of experience, develop professional standards of conduct, and prevent misunderstandings between employees about the institution's philosophy and goals.

General Training

All too often, correctional personnel enter service with little or no training. This lack of training, together with no prior experience, can be a volatile combination in a correctional institution. Inexperienced officers simply cannot be expected to deal with serious crises as wisely and effectively as more seasoned staff. The result can be disastrous, as demonstrated in the case of

the 1980 New Mexico riot, in which a lack of experienced officers on the scene at the onset of the disturbance contributed to one of several serious errors in the institution's management the evening the disturbance began.

For these reasons, a comprehensive, well-organized training program is an essential part of every correctional institution. Special consideration must be given to developing practical pre-assignment training programs for new employees, instead of assigning new staff to a post with little or no formal training. New

To attract the quality personnel necessary in a correctional institution, heavy emphasis must be placed on adequate salaries and satisfactory working conditions.

employees in the past (and in some locations even today) were assigned to a post with a brief orientation and little else. In some instances they were paired with a more experienced officer for a brief period. But in many cases, they received no systematic training in institutional procedures, inmate characteristics, emergency procedures, or other critical knowledge areas. This lack of training, together with a deficit in correctional experience, can be a volatile combination in a correctional institution.

The standards of the ACA Commission on Accreditation for Corrections require that new correctional officers receive 160 hours of training during their first year and 40 hours each year thereafter as long as they have contact with inmates.[1] A training curriculum for new staff in accord with these standards is often taught at a separate staff training center or academy. In addition to the initial familiarization training given at the local institution, a formal agency training program can expose them to the policies and basic procedures specific to that agency. In many cases, successful completion of formal academy training is required for an employee to be retained by an agency.

In addition to pre-assignment or academy training for new personnel, an ongoing staff-development program for employees at all levels should be a requirement for all correctional systems. Such a program ordinarily provides for the continuing personal and professional development of all staff. The additional exposure to specific operational subjects, including riot procedures and control, is an important part of this annual refresher training.

Supervisory Training

One important area that is often overlooked is supervisory or managerial training. Although the focus of this manual is riots and disturbances (and certainly staff training should include these topics), a broader program for top staff is important as well. To the degree that institutional managers are able to develop their native skills and acquire others, they will be far better equipped to manage the institution on a daily basis. From that ability will flow an improved institutional climate, which will itself dampen the

---

[1]Appendix B contains relevant standards.

tensions and inevitable stresses that are often core components in institutional disturbances. Crisis management and riot and hostage situation simulations can be useful in managerial training that prepares top staff to deal with a riot or disturbance.

Riot Training

Emergency training for line staff is of utmost importance. All employees should be thoroughly familiar with the riot plan and be required to review it frequently. Their proficiency in the use of emergency equipment and firearms and their overall knowledge of the plan are critical to an effective response in a crisis. Accordingly, training in riot control principles and tactics should be a part of entry-level training for all staff, as well as annual refresher training. In most systems, all security staff are potential squad members, and in a number of agencies, all staff are. Ideally, all employees should be trained in these skills, not just specific response team members. However, staff who have special weapons or equipment qualifications should be pre-identified, and issue of those items should be limited to them only.

Training of this type should include, at a minimum: use of emergency keys for access to every area; familiarity with entrance routes; tactical squad response options and formations; and use of gas and smoke munitions and equipment, including gas masks. Control center officers must be trained in all aspects of the response system, as well as the members of the emergency response squads. Hypothetical case studies and drills are good strategies to use in these training programs.

All personnel authorized to use firearms must receive appropriate training that covers their use, safety, care, and limits on their use. They must demonstrate firearm proficiency on at least an annual basis, and the institution should retain records of these qualification tests. Furthermore, each facility should have a system for assigning only these properly qualified staff to armed posts.

Staff should also receive specific training in the use of gas guns, grenades, and other devices before being permitted to use them. Used in the wrong way, or the wrong circumstances, these munitions can be just as deadly as a standard firearm.

Emergency Response Teams

Almost all institutions provide basic emergency response training to all staff, including squad formations and tactics. However, many institutions have a special emergency response team, which is trained specifically to respond to institutional crises such as fights, riots, forced cell moves, and hostage situations.

These employees are almost always selected according to written criteria and receive additional training in squad tactics, use of special weapons, and other emergency reaction strategies. These staff may be on call throughout the day by radio, and may even carry pagers when off duty so they can be quickly recalled to the institution during non-duty hours. Appendix C contains suggested basic qualification information for such a team.

2

Underlying Contributors to Disturbances

Prison disturbances are complex and varied in their origins. But it is well known that underlying systemic and institutional factors such as overcrowding, idleness, inadequate security, lack of staff, poor staff training, substandard facilities, and lack of programs can contribute to these crisis events. Even so, it is not possible to identify a specific cause, or set of causes, that will always precipitate a disturbance, or the absence of which will always prevent one. Although many disturbances seem to have been caused by a simple, critical episode, those incidents are often just sparks igniting an already volatile, riot-prone situation. Nonetheless, in many cases, a causal relationship can be identified between one or more of the variables discussed in this chapter and most major disturbances in U.S. prisons.

An important but little-discussed aspect of disturbances is the female inmate issue. This is largely because the incarceration of an increasing number of female inmates is an emerging correctional trend in America today, but the incidence of full-fledged disturbances in female institutions is quite low. For that reason, this publication focuses primarily on the origins of, and tactics generally used to deal with, such incidents in male facilities. However, administrators of female institutions should also be alert to the conditions and precursor events described in sections below, and be equally prepared to deal with budding problems that could grow to major proportions if not properly managed. "It never happened before" will be a poor substitute for advance preparation should a

major disturbance ever occur in a female correctional institution.

INSTITUTIONAL ENVIRONMENT

A correctional institution is, by its very nature, an unnatural environment, one that invariably contributes to inmates' emotional stress level. Most institutions have, as part of the day-to-day environment, regimentation and limited personal freedom, lack of privacy, sexual deprivation, separation from family and friends, and many similar sources of emotional stress.

These stresses can easily reach explosive levels when other aggravating elements are added to prisons' monotony and boredom. They may include such factors as: substandard and overcrowded physical space, poor or monotonous food, brutality, racial conflicts and gang activity, unfair or capricious treatment, and poor management, security, and supervision.

SUBSTANDARD FACILITIES

Many riots have occurred in aging, overcrowded institutions, and, unfortunately, inmates are still held in such facilities today throughout America. Administrators of these prisons are faced with the problem of making necessary improvements in the existing physical plant in order to mitigate these adverse conditions to the extent possible.

It should be noted, however, that riots are not confined to outmoded facilities alone;

disturbances have also occurred in some modern institutions. To a large extent, though, an institution's physical inadequacy is a major contributing factor that can lead to disturbances. It certainly shapes the course of disruptions once they begin. People are responsive to their physical environment. In the view of many experts, there is little doubt that physical conditions are almost always part of the underlying causes of riots, if not the major factor.

Long-standing practices in the architectural design of correctional institutions, and the related concepts of efficiency and functionality, have contributed to the dehumanization of the prison environment. Long corridors, repeated doorways, highly polished floors, and hard finishes can be hypnotic and can result in the depersonalization of surroundings. Furthermore, cells frequently face blank walls, paved courtyards, and a treeless landscape. The result can be an institutional environment that lacks stimulation and variation, producing adverse effects in the inmate population over time.

An institution's physical inadequacy is a major contributing factor that can lead to disturbances.

Many of these antiquated facilities have been poorly maintained; some were built before 1900, and their inherently repressive atmosphere affects both staff and inmates. Plumbing, heating, lighting, and ventilation are frequently inadequate. Soundproofing is often nonexistent. The result is that thousands of inmates live in an environment that is not only uncomfortable, but can be relatively unhealthy. In addition, these outmoded facilities often cannot support the level of programs and services needed by inmates and increasingly expected by the courts and society.

And so, to the depressing physical surroundings is added a lack of treatment programs, which can increase emotional tensions and sometimes contribute to major disturbances.

Fortunately, successful renovation of even the most antiquated facilities is possible; fine examples exist in Georgia State Prison, Reidsville, Ga., and the U.S. Penitentiary, Leavenworth, Kan. Renovations can and should include improved cell space and cell fixtures, better ventilation and lighting, and improvements in program areas, particularly recreation and visiting.

As institutions increase in design or adapted size, the ability of management to control the population is often decreased, and the results in many cases are predictable. Small, well-designed institutions with individual cells certainly are much more effective in reducing these adverse factors. However, large, overcrowded, poorly designed correctional institutions with open dormitories are the realities that most correctional administrators live with. Therefore, administrators in those settings must be constantly seeking innovative methods for improving institutional facilities to neutralize these effects to the greatest extent possible. But the adaptive work at Reidsville and Leavenworth shows how even large, unwieldy cellhouses and dormitories can be recycled into smaller, highly functional housing areas that are far easier to supervise and less dehumanizing.

There is a second fundamental factor in the area of outmoded facilities. In addition to the psychological impact on inmates, the physical plant can have a tremendous predisposing influence on the origins and course of a riot. Massive, hard-to-supervise cellblocks, poorly configured perimeters, and the lack of appropriate modern security hardware can create conditions ripe for inmate exploitation. Moreover,

the layout of most older facilities makes prompt, effective responses somewhat more difficult, and thus may enhance the rioters' advantage in important ways, both at the flash point of the event as well as during a siege or assault by staff to retake the facility. While new, more modern designs remedy some of these problems, they must not be forgotten in the course of renovations and other institutional changes over the years. One ever-present problem will be the fact that the very security features that make it difficult for an inmate to escape also tend to make it difficult for staff to regain control in a riot.

INADEQUATE FUNDING

No single factor is most important in considering the causes of institutional disturbances, but inadequate financing is an underlying cause in many, if not most. Hand-to-mouth budget practices and deficit financing, usually stemming from political considerations, are at the root of many of the personnel, physical plant, and program deficiencies that set the stage for major problems of this type.

OVERCROWDING

Hand in hand with antiquated facilities, prison overcrowding has been a major ongoing concern for the last decade. The U.S. prison population continues to climb, and there is every indication that it will do so for the foreseeable future (Potter 1980 and Bureau of Justice Statistics 1989).

In many prisons, two or more inmates are forced to live in cells designed for only one, or in dormitories when, instead, they should be more properly housed in cells. Dayrooms, corridors, and other common areas are being pressed into service for inmate housing in most institutions. Toilets, showers, and other communal facilities are shared by numbers far beyond their intended capacities.

Under these conditions, the tendency to violent eruption increases dramatically. Not only do interpersonal tensions in housing units rise, but predatory inmates are more likely to exploit these conditions, further increasing inmate-inmate animosities and group tensions. Moreover, support facilities, such as gymnasiums, kitchens, dining rooms, industries, and medical facilities, all become increasingly stressed as the number of beds added to a fixed-capacity institution rises. In many institutions, program resources have simply become inadequate for the increased numbers of inmates they must serve.

STAFFING LEVELS

Furthermore, as populations rise, inmate/staff ratios inevitably increase. This results in reduced supervision levels and access to personal services, depersonalization, inadequate security, and additional stress in many institutions. The absence of effective administrative remedies for grievances, implementation of new determinate sentencing structures with no parole, and a well-publicized get-tough public mindset all add to a feeling of alienation and general helplessness on the part of many inmates. It is not difficult to envision how certain inmates might react to the combined depersonalization of the human and physical environment through planned or spontaneous violence.

IDLENESS AND LACK OF PROGRAMMING

Idleness associated with overcrowding is a critical component of not only riot situations, but also a great many lesser but still serious internal management problems. Constructive programs and meaningful activities are methods that have proved successful in many institutions in reducing idleness and the tensions that can predispose an inmate population to aggressive protests or outright violence. Astute administrators are sure to have some kind of very visible project going on at all times to improve inmate-related conditions. These might include renovating the visiting room, housing, or recreation areas; adding more inmate telephones; or taking some other morale-boosting action to show that the administration cares about basic living conditions in the institution.

It has long been recognized that interesting and satisfying work is an important factor in maintaining emotional stability. Prison industries are a particularly valuable program, but other meaningful activities should be sought for the institutional population as well. Whatever the program, administrators should seek to generate viable alternatives to forced idleness, so as to preempt the rise in tensions associated with it.

PUBLIC APATHY

The public is often concerned only with having convicted offenders imprisoned, thus removing what is considered to be a disruptive or dangerous agent from society. The public sentiment toward drug offenders that is currently sweeping the nation clearly has this flavor. With such a mindset, there is little citizen concern for treatment methods and policies in correctional institutions. This attitude often pervades the institution, and the inmates react to it in a variety of deeply ingrained, negative ways that can set the stage for a disturbance. One reaction is apathy within the institutional population itself, with inmates showing little motivation or enthusiasm toward participating in treatment programs or cooperating with staff. Another can be a feeling of further alienation, as inmates see themselves increasingly defined as outcasts from society, and lose confidence in their ability to successfully return to a larger society.

Correctional staff can also be affected by public apathy. With little or no support from the community, it is a continuous challenge for correctional administrators to maintain staff morale and implement realistic programs. Moreover, public support translates into resources. While for the first time in many years there appears to be a recognition that additional resources are needed for correctional construction, there is little discussion about the programming vitally necessary to support these new beds. Moreover, the proportionally greater, ongoing operational costs of the construction currently envisioned are staggering and should be addressed in future government planning.

Thus, the challenge for administrators today is to effectively convey the need for a balanced approach to correctional practices. They must seek an administrative posture that indeed safeguards the community, but at the same time offers inmates at least a ray of hope during confinement. And this support must be built in such a way as to ensure ongoing resources at a level heretofore unheard of in our society.

PUNITIVE ATTITUDES

In an era of increasing violent and drug-related crimes, it is not surprising that society responds by demanding punishment and retribution. Line personnel often reflect this attitude of punishment, as opposed to treatment. When this occurs, inmates find little sympathy for their plight—real or imagined—from either the public or staff. This punitive attitude on the part of a large segment of society can be another factor that underlies many major disturbances.

To operate effectively as an agent of society,

the correctional administrator must find a balanced philosophy and convey it to staff at every level. It is the administrator's job to understand the community's punitive attitude, and yet to recruit and train a staff that can be trained to be committed to the positive values of correctional treatment. Administrators must use in-service training to educate the staff as to the philosophical balance favored by the agency, and how the goals of the institution implement that balance.

INEQUITIES IN THE CRIMINAL JUSTICE SYSTEM

One frequent cause of inmate unrest is the disparity in sentencing practices of various courts. States that have indeterminate sentencing laws and central boards that fix definite terms and grant paroles have the least difficulty from this source. The problem of disparity of sentences is further complicated by the old adage that money buys a good attorney, so the rich go free and the

> *No single factor is most important in considering the causes of institutional disturbances, but inadequate financing is an underlying cause in many, if not most.*

poor are sentenced to prison. Thus, inmates often look at themselves as members of a poor underclass, whose very sentences are a symbol of societal inequities.

The complexity of the criminal justice system and the existence of inflexible legislative restrictions in some jurisdictions can add to the appearance of inequality. These elements are generally beyond the scope of correctional administrators to change. However, the fact remains that perceived inequities in the criminal justice system are a source of problems for the correctional administrator. It is human to excuse and rationalize one's own behavior and displace anger; in this instance, the prison system is a logical scapegoat. For inmates who experience these tensions, the institution and its staff are simply the only available outlet for this hostility.

Once again, a special case example for this dynamic is the Atlanta/Oakdale disturbances. The detainees had very direct and strongly held feelings of frustration about the immigration process, and the way they felt they had been treated by the U.S. Immigration and Naturalization Service (INS). They evidently believed that the INS staff represented all that was wrong with the system. Accordingly, they targeted the INS building at Oakdale for destruction, and at both locations sought unsuccessfully to take INS staff hostages. Conversely, they did not harbor these resentments toward the Bureau of Prisons staff who actually ran the institution; while they were threatened and physically intimidated periodically, Bureau staff were not harmed seriously (with the exception of an attack by a mentally deranged detainee on one officer).

In summary, the direct and indirect causes of many institutional disturbances lie in complex, sometimes interrelated factors. To the degree that institutional administrators are aware of them, and take proper steps to remedy those factors within their power, the institution will be far safer and less likely to experience a major disruption.

3

Direct Causes of Disturbances

The makeup of the inmate population cannot be overlooked as a basic cause of disturbances. Correctional institutions in the United States are populated primarily by young, unmarried males who are from the lower social and economic strata of society. They are frequently the products of broken homes, poorly educated and unskilled, with unstable work records. They also are apt to have a prior criminal record and low self-esteem and be uncommitted to any major goals in life. Material failure in a culture firmly oriented toward success is the common denominator of most inmate populations.

Interestingly, despite the fact that many inmates have committed serious violations of the law, most tend to be reasonably responsible members of the institutional community. Generally, they want the prison to run smoothly and for their lives to be as pleasant and safe as possible under the circumstances. No one stands to lose more in a riot situation than the inmates. They have the greatest risk of being injured or killed or of having their property damaged or destroyed. In most riots almost all inmates want the situation resolved as quickly as possible.

There are, however, subgroups within the general prison population of most institutions that are, for a variety of reasons, especially prone to causing problems that may erupt in violence and disorder.

INMATE GROUPS PRONE TO CAUSING PROBLEMS

Antisocial Inmates

Some inmates are sociopaths—angry at society and lacking in what are considered normal societal values. They are prone to wanton destruction of property and injury to others. Frequently scheming to overthrow authority—as represented in prison society by the administration—they go to great lengths to identify and exploit security breaches. They become astute students of every aspect of the physical plant, as well as institutional operations. Since they spend 24 hours each day in the institution, their knowledge of security procedures and weaknesses can easily exceed that of administrative staff. Such inmates are a significant concern.

These inmates also comprise a large percentage of the population in locked units, and the risks presented by a concentration of this category in these relatively small units cannot be overlooked. In addition, the release of such inmates from locked units is often the objective of rioters during a widespread disturbance. Adequate procedural and physical safeguards must be in place to prevent the release of these volatile inmates, many of whom would in all likelihood feed the already violent atmosphere of a disturbance.

Inmates with Mental Problems

A significant number of inmates can be diagnosed as psychopaths, or as having other serious mental health conditions. Some commonly accepted characteristics of the psychopath are: an inability to develop meaningful interpersonal relationships; the absence of a conscience; a need for immediate gratification; low frustration levels; and an inability to learn from experience. These inmates are frequently hard to understand and manage, especially by correctional staff who have not had appropriate training in the mental health area.

The problem is complicated by a small number of inmates who experience psychotic episodes, in which they lose contact with reality. In some cases they can become very dangerous because their behavior is so unpredictable and bizarre. They, too, have a tendency to disturb or create unrest in the remainder of the inmate population. To the extent that institutional and agency procedures permit, these inmates should be segregated from the institution's main population and procedures initiated to transfer them to a mental health facility.

Correctional institutions also have a disproportionate share of individuals who are mentally deficient, emotionally unstable, and prone to violent and other socially deviant behavior. These inmates, while not certifiably mentally ill, often are part of the nucleus of a group of troublemakers. Through their erratic, unpredictable, or aggressive actions, they can be the spark that ignites an institution already predisposed toward a disturbance.

Racial/Ethnic Minorities

Racial/ethnic minority groups are grossly overrepresented in the nation's prisons as compared to society at large. At the end of 1987 (the last year for which full figures are available), approximately 34 percent of the U.S. prison population were black, whereas in the nation as a whole, the black population amounts to only about 12 percent. Similarly, Hispanics are overrepresented in the prison population in many states. As a result, minority inmates often view themselves as political inmates, victimized by an unjust society.

Racial and ethnic lines are frequently even more firmly drawn in correctional institutions than in the community. Racial identity therefore may lead to the formation of prison gangs and other special inmate groups competing for power and control—sometimes resulting in violence and disturbances.

Prison Gangs

Correctional administrators have watched with great concern the emergence in the last decade of prison gangs as a moving force in many facilities. Extortion, drugs, assaults, murders, and staff intimidation are the trademark of the prison gang. Direct confrontations between opposing groups are not unknown, creating extremely hazardous conditions.

But even when their activities are less immediately threatening, these groups tend to polarize significant numbers of inmates. Their activities create tensions over prison drug trafficking, which they attempt to control, and otherwise create background conditions that are ripe for creating wider disruptions.

Such gangs are frequently formed along racial or ethnic lines. Groups of this type include the Mexican Mafia, Aryan Brotherhood, Nuestra Familia, Black Guerilla Family, and Texas Syndicate. Others are increasingly becoming politicized, or have taken on the outward form of a religion in an attempt to obtain some First Amendment protection for their activities. The best known of these groups is the El Rukn group in Illinois state prisons, whose members spring from a Chicago street gang.

Originally, the purpose for forming many prison gangs appears to have been self-protection.

In recent years, however, gang-oriented activities have led to brutal killings and "wars," often over drug trafficking. Some gangs have now extended their influence into surrounding communities, and in some instances appear to be making efforts to compete with more traditional organized crime (Kahn & Zinn 1979).

In addition to the internal tension and violence associated with prison gang activity, gang members and their outside associates place indirect and sometimes direct pressure on staff. Threats and intimidation sometimes extend to employees' families. Staff who have been compromised or undermined in their professional resolve by these tactics become weak links that can be exploited. These employees also may be the weak link that breaks during a minor disturbance, permitting it to develop into a full-blown riot. Thus, prison gang members need special attention in a prison setting.

In order to effectively combat this growing menace, a comprehensive intelligence-gathering system should be in place. Telephone monitoring, correspondence tracking, and other techniques have been successful in interdicting many planned gang activities. Other response strategies have ranged from confining all confirmed gang members in one institution, to segregating members of different gangs in different institutions, to permitting a normal population mixture but devoting increased attention to the actions of individual gang members and segregating them on the basis of individual rule infractions. Whatever the approach—and there is no agreement on which is best—the serious potential for violence presented by this group cannot be overlooked.

In most riots almost all inmates want the situation resolved as quickly as possible.

Radical/Revolutionary Organizations

The antisocial attitudes of many inmates, as well as the tendency of many of them to view themselves as political prisoners, have made them an easy, high-priority target for recruitment by revolutionary organizations. Evidence suggests that some of these organizations have attempted to infiltrate and influence existing prison gangs. These efforts appear to involve training gang members in terrorist tactics and in gaining sympathy for political philosophies. Acts of terrorism have become more frequent inside correctional institutions, and have on occasion reached outside as well. Certainly not the least serious example of this was a plot several years ago to kidnap the children of California correctional officers.

It is not appropriate to include in this manual a list of specific terrorist organizations known to exist in correctional institutions. However, a comprehensive intelligence system is a vitally important tool in combatting this divisive element in many institutions. Prison staff should certainly be aware, however, through their intelligence-gathering system, of any revolutionary organizations that might have contact with their inmates. These same analyses can be used to identify the signs of gang activity and pinpoint the indicators of individual gang membership, such as tattoos.

PRINCIPLES OF COLLECTIVE BEHAVIOR

Inmates as a whole have difficulty sharing goals and objectives, and they are unlikely to unite over anything but the strongest issues. The 1987 Oakdale/Atlanta disturbances seem to prove the second aspect of this point. For almost two weeks, at two separate institutions that were in total inmate control, the rioters held to a single set of demands, effectively protected more than 125 hostages from almost all physical harm, and negotiated a unified agreement. The threat of repatriation to Cuba was evidently such a strong motivating factor for every detainee that they were able to act in unison to a great extent. This clearly is not typical in most institutions, where the different types of inmates ordinarily are not able to cooperate for long periods.

However, when inmates become frustrated, fearful, or otherwise feel they have been aggrieved, agitators do have a much easier time getting even normal nonparticipants to join in aggressive acts. But the leadership dynamics of an ongoing disturbance appear to shift over time, in many cases. Although it is not unusual for an inmate leader to command a modest following of loyal supporters, it is unusual for such a leader to control an entire institution for any length of time, particularly during the dynamic pressures of a disturbance.[1]

When tension builds before a disturbance, there is frequently considerable emotional contagion. Rumors tend to become rampant and can turn a crowd into a "mob." At such times, measures intended to prevent or to take prudent precautions against a budding disturbance— sirens, news helicopters, fire engines, etc.—may increase the excitement level. When emotionally stimulated by inmate leaders, or when faced with what they believe to be an impending crisis of staff making, inmates might experience an unusual sense of group unity while losing their sense of individual self-discipline. When this occurs and the other factors mentioned above are in place, the climate can be ripe for a disturbance.

FEAR OF VIOLENCE AS A CAUSATIVE FACTOR

Fear of inmate-on-inmate violence is pervasive within some correctional institutions, and can be one of the predisposing conditions for a riot or disturbance. Ironically, the most effective strategies for reducing this factor can also create other problems. If inmates are totally isolated and confined from each other, violence and mass action are essentially precluded, but both mental

When tension builds before a disturbance, there is frequently considerable emotional contagion.

and social problems develop. On the other hand, if inmates are allowed to mingle, occasional violence is almost inevitable. Effective security and supervision, then, must be the key to a balanced response to this issue.

Unfortunately, budget constraints often result in inmate/staff ratios that make it difficult to provide continuous supervision throughout an institution. Moreover, antiquated physical plants hamper direct staff supervision. So, to the degree staff are unwilling or unable to protect them, inmates often use their own resources to try to bolster their feeling of safety from others, and that can include fabricating and carrying weapons and taking other steps that have violent undertones.

Some of these fears are well-founded, because

---

[1]The Oakdale/Atlanta example demonstrates this again, because throughout the two weeks the leadership structure shifted on several occasions. Given the length of time involved, and the volatility of the situation, this is not surprising. Even up to the final stages of negotiations on a settlement, dissenting groups and competing leaders were a factor.

unfortunately, even with the best inmate classification systems, there is always a subgroup of most aggressive inmates in every population—inmates who will prey on others if given the opportunity. These more aggressive inmates tend to use threats and force to achieve their ends—sexual activity, drugs, or other favors. And so it is not unusual for problems to materialize even in well-managed facilities, and for many less aggressive inmates to live in constant fear. As a result some may improvise weapons in an attempt to protect themselves.

Thus, a portion of the violence within institutions is a result of outright aggression, and a portion is traceable to these frightened individuals attempting to protect themselves from abuse by other inmates. Either way, an atmosphere of fear—where inmates feel staff are not in control and inmates are—leads to a base level of violence, tension, and fear that can be at the root of a disturbance.

INCIDENT-RELATED CAUSES

Given the many possible underlying conditions that can be in place in a given institution, it can take only a small incident to

A spontaneous security breach can be just as great a danger as a repetitive one.

trigger a disturbance. Two circumstances are often found to be behind major incidents: a security breach by staff that inmates take advantage of in a planned or spontaneous action and the random incident.

Security Breaches

Considerable attention has been paid in most correctional institutions to establishing security procedures that prevent or reduce the baseline conditions that breed disturbances. In fact, on a day-to-day basis, these preventive elements are far more important to pursue than active training in riot formations, use of chemical agents, or other direct skills.

The sad fact is that in too many institutions, fundamental security procedures are inadequate or, if adequate, they are not adequately followed.

Inmates readily become aware of security breaches, and there are always a few inmates in every institution who will try to take advantage of them. Sound security procedures must be established and then continuously monitored to ensure compliance. Inmates quickly learn when a particular staff member does not lock a grille, or carries a set of keys into a restricted area. And in many instances, these staff shortcuts have enabled inmates to launch a major disturbance. It is only through constant supervisory attention to every detail that this ongoing risk factor will be eliminated.

A spontaneous security breach can be just as great a danger as a repetitive one. A staff member carrying the wrong key into the wrong area just once, or leaving a grille open at a critical moment, can be seized on by alert inmates who then attempt a takeover. Supervisory staff must constantly impress on staff the need to never let such a slip occur.

The Random Incident

A disturbance is sometimes caused by a random incident that gets out of control and sows the seeds of discontent in an inmate population. An inmate who is being taken to segregation draws a crowd; a staff member momentarily loses self-control and hits an inmate; an inmates "goes off" and assaults a staff member, takes keys, and incites others. These trigger events may be tied to some other circumstance, or they may be totally unanticipated, even in the best-managed facilities.

The available course of action in such instances is to quickly and professionally contain the scene of the disruptive event, treat the inmate or inmates involved as professionally as possible, and deal openly and fairly with any staff misconduct that may be involved. Administrators should maintain an open line of communication with the inmate population in the aftermath of

such an event, while discreetly preparing contingency plans and response forces if tension appears to be building.

NONINSTITUTIONAL CAUSES

Correctional administrators must be aware of the conditions and practices within the institution that may precipitate a disturbance. They also must be aware of causes *outside* the institution that may create tension and hostility in the institution, which can trigger a serious incident. Prisons continue to feel the impact of unrest in the larger community. Administrators must be constantly aware of the disruptive influence of social strife, militant movements, and various kinds of civil disorders on inmates. Even though many institutions are physically remote, they are not isolated. Reports in the press and on radio and television keep inmates well informed of unrest in the larger community. Broader visiting, telephone, and correspondence policies permit other avenues of information to enter the institution.

In short, correctional facilities no longer operate in a vacuum, and the management implications of that fact are significant. Specific events can increase base-level tensions and trigger internal unrest. Administrators have a responsibility to be sensitive to noninstitutional factors that may heighten tensions, and to do what they can to neutralize their impact on the inmate population. As will be noted later, this factor was a key missing ingredient in the start of the Oakdale/Atlanta disturbances.

In some cases, it also is appropriate to take an affirmative approach through the media to getting out a message about these events. Whether this is an effective option or not largely depends on the disposition of the local media and the credibility of the correctional administrator with media representatives.

4

General Disturbance Prevention

Many factors seem beyond the control of correctional administrators—overcrowding, lack of funds, public attitudes, and legislation. These elements, however, can be recognized and their effects on institutions understood. The correctional administrator certainly should not abdicate responsibility in these areas. Part of the job includes a sound public relations program that informs the public of needed correctional programs, develops a constituency for corrections, and makes a strong appeal for sufficient funds to satisfactorily operate institutions. Another part is keeping the inmate population abreast of how such changes may affect day-to-day life in the institution and reducing rumors and associated unrest. Awareness of these areas implies that conscientious staff will seek preventive measures as well.

Prevention has two distinct meanings. First, it refers to all the fundamental steps that can and should be taken to ensure that an institution is well administered. This includes providing a sanitary, safe, and humane environment and respecting the rights of both inmates and staff. Prevention also refers to a more active mode: detecting and correcting problem conditions, as well as the signs of mounting tensions, and finding effective means of defusing volatile situations in time to forestall violence and disorder.

SENSITIVITY TO THE SIGNS OF TENSION

Disturbances in correctional institutions can be prevented by staff who are able to detect, interpret, and act on changes in the institutional atmosphere and inmate behavior patterns. Experienced institutional personnel can sense, in most cases, a change in the general climate of the institution. Among the more obvious signs of such a change are: unusually quiet or subdued actions by inmate groups; reluctance to communicate with employees; increased purchases of foodstuffs at inmate stores; unusual inmate gatherings or increased self-segregation by racial or ethnic groups; appearance of inflammatory written material; an increase in voluntary lockups; a drop in attendance at movies or other popular functions; and an increase in complaints about some operations of the institution. (For a more detailed list, see Appendix D.)

Prevention obviously entails placing the most alert and effective employees in the most critical areas of the institution, areas involving security as well as inmate morale. Line personnel are the first to hear complaints about food, mail delays, and unpopular management actions, providing inmates feel free to talk to them. If employees' lines of communication with supervisors are open, these complaints can be transmitted upward so that corrective action can be taken.

When tensions are mounting, employees must use restraint and discretion, to avoid aggravating the situation. During these tense times, an appearance of assured control and confidence

can reduce tension greatly. Additional staff may be placed in key areas to facilitate communications with the inmate population. If new employees become unduly alarmed about a routine matter, this can be an opportunity for constructive on-the-job training. Line personnel who give signs of not being capable of maintaining their composure and professionalism should be temporarily placed in less sensitive areas, if possible, or given supportive assistance and encouragement. In general, a restrained response is thought to be the best course of action in a time of increased tension.[1]

IMPROVEMENT OF EXISTING FACILITIES

Obviously, a new, well-designed institution should be easier to manage from a security standpoint than an old, outmoded design. However, in the absence of new facilities, significant improvements of old structures can be accomplished with a fairly limited budget and a good plan. If carried out correctly, appropriate renovations could be a significant riot prevention measure. The following are but a few suggestions for such improvements.

Painting is an important element of any such plan; old traditional colors, or cracked and peeling paint, set a negative tone for the institution. Although it is cosmetic, fresh paint can be psychologically significant. Color can change the apparent size of a cell and bring relief into the confining monotony of an individual inmate's life. It can brighten the atmosphere and improve the light level in housing units and cells.

Poor lighting is a related source of inmate complaints. The quality of light—including the surfaces that reflect it and the shadows it makes—is as important to consider as the quantity of light. A simple increase of light intensity is not necessarily an improvement, from

---

[1]However, an interesting counterpoint to this conventional wisdom is found in the Oakdale/Atlanta disturbances. Cuban detainees in those institutions had previously been steeped in a "macho" culture, and many of them had been held in Cuban prisons, where overt force was a daily response to inmate unrest. These detainees interpreted the Bureau of Prisons' communication strategy and veiled response forces as a sign of weakness and lack of resolve on the part of the administration. The Bureau response did not, in fact, constitute a weak posture, but unwittingly this low-key strategy may have emboldened the detainee leadership in the pre-disturbance period, enabled them to convince wavering inmates that a takeover was possible, and indeed may have been a significant factor in the origins of the uprisings. The lesson is that even the most conventional response strategies must be tailored to the specific events and inmates involved.

Many disturbances may be

prevented if both staff and

inmates know exactly what is

expected of them, what is

allowed, and what the other

party thinks and feels.

the inmate's viewpoint. In many cases, however, it is obvious that more and better lighting is needed.

One relatively recent innovation in lighting technology is the use of light sources that provide a full spectrum of light waves, as found naturally outdoors from the sun, and reflected natural light. Studies have demonstrated that full-spectrum artificial light sources used indoors provide a number of mental and physical health benefits, including improved biological functioning and more positive attitudes. The benefits of full-

spectrum artificial light sources are much greater than those from the more common "cold" (partial spectrum) light tubes or bulbs.

Another obvious area needing urgent attention in most old correctional institutions is the plumbing facilities. In some cases, communal showers and toilets and cell toilets have become repulsive with neglect. New epoxies and other plastic finishes can be used in these areas. This not only improves appearances and reduces noxious odors, but prevents concealment of contraband. Advice from fire authorities should be sought to determine whether fire and smoke propagation qualities of these materials are within acceptable limits.

High noise levels are an inevitable factor in many older institutional designs, and they are a common source of irritation to both inmates and staff. As in the case of lighting, and the new plastics and epoxies, there is a wide range of relatively inexpensive soundproofing materials that can address this problem. But even before these are considered, the use of simple rubber bumpers in doors and gates can greatly reduce this common noise source. The skillful application of appropriate soundproofing surfaces can go far to reduce much of the remaining noise pollution in old cellblocks. In many cases, the soundproofing project could be used in

connection with new paint to improve the overall atmosphere of the institution at a relatively low cost.

In making any of these modifications, fireproofing and fire prevention should be considered. Almost all new materials of this kind are manufactured with this important factor in mind, but this cannot be assumed, and safety ratings should be checked. At the same time, there should be an examination of the amount of "fuel" materials already present in the institution; any reasonable reduction should be undertaken.

Another adverse environmental factor in housing areas is the lack of adequate ventilation, which reduces personal comfort. Thick exterior walls, in many cases bordering small concrete paved courts, absorb solar heat, which is re-radiated during the evening hours, creating temperatures above the comfort level. With overcrowding and inadequate air exchange, body odors compounded by toilet odors can create stifling conditions. The addition of fans to move air through exhausts and to change air at acceptable rates is the only remedy for these conditions in older facilities, where other renovation costs would be prohibitive.

STAFF VISIBILITY

Numerous informal contacts will give management a better idea of the general institutional mood than will any number of formal reports. For that reason, administrative personnel, from the chief executive officer to the first-level counselors and supervisors, should be highly visible, circulating throughout the institution, maintaining as much contact as possible with inmates and employees. These contacts will serve to answer questions and relieve the anxieties and tensions of both inmates and line employees. At least one nationwide study has found that there were fewer disturbances in institutions where high-level administrators made themselves available in housing units to communicate with both inmates and staff.

These kinds of contacts also facilitate crisis responses, when they are necessary. They provide top staff with more in-depth knowledge of institutional programs and procedures, and the inmates and staff themselves. When decisions must be made during a disturbance, this additional dimension of knowledge about the institution can make the difference between a good decision and a bad one.

Another, often unrecognized benefit is the degree of familiarity that these contacts give staff and inmates with the administrators' personal

and professional traits. If the line staff has seen the top management regularly deal openly and fairly with them, then they will have a much higher level of confidence in management decisions during a crisis. As to inmates, the middle of a disturbance is not the time for staff to try to establish credibility with a group of mutineers; the observations inmates make about top staff in daily contacts can be the key deciding factor at such times.

EFFECTIVE COMMUNICATION

In order to manage security within modern institutions, an effective interpersonal communication system must be maintained. Such a system allows for a variety of methods by which staff can effectively learn institution policy before it is disseminated to the inmate population.

From one perspective, a riot or disturbance is a form of communication—a dramatic one that is seldom used unless other forms of communications have been tried and failed. Open channels of communication, both formal and informal, permit valuable information to become available to staff for making decisions and

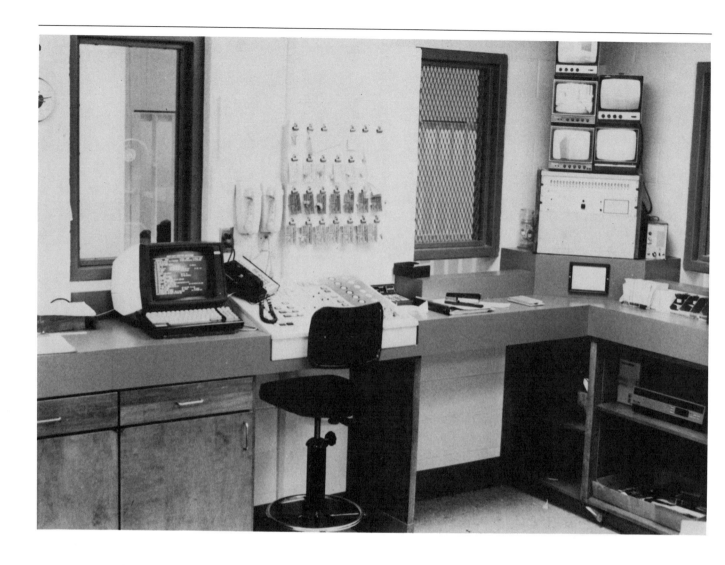

policies. They also permit institutional policy and procedure to be made clear to staff and inmates. Many disturbances may be prevented if both staff and inmates know exactly what is expected of them, what is allowed, and what the other party thinks and feels. This requires a climate where inmates and employees alike can express constructive opinions and feelings without meeting defensiveness or fearing later reprisal.

Correctional officers and work supervisors are the staff members who have the most contact with inmates; their knowledge and competence are of utmost importance in maintaining the day-to-day flow of information in an institution. Since inmates rely on line personnel for interpretation of administrative directives, it is imperative that staff in these categories be well informed and able to fulfill this responsibility. Inmates and staff should receive reliable, official information about programs and policies, particularly when changes are to be made or new policies instituted. There is nothing more demoralizing to staff than to hear of policy changes for the institution through rumors or from inmates. When inmates lack facts,

rumors take their place, and misinformation is spread throughout the institution, which can lead to unrest and disorder. Clearly written policies and procedures made available to staff and inmates are an important form of communication that can prevent this dynamic from creating major problems.

As a result, administrators must remember the importance of staff training and familiarity with the rules and regulations, and the value of briefing employees on changes that may be immediately forthcoming. To prevent dangerous daily gaps in the information system that can grow to serious proportions, it is very important to ensure a full exchange of information from one shift to another. It is important for the relieving officer to have a good understanding of the current situation when coming on duty. The safety of the institution, as well as the officer, may well be determined by this kind of information. Carefully kept logs, roll calls, and post orders should be augmented as needed with verbal briefings. This information should include, but not be limited to, unit activities, inmate

> *Collecting intelligence data should be a day-to-day operation, with staff from every part of the institution and every level of the organization involved.*

information, institutional facts and events, and a review of any confidential log information on noteworthy or potentially dangerous inmates.

SPECIFIC INTELLIGENCE-GATHERING ACTIVITY

Reliable information, systematically collected and analyzed, is vitally important in preventing riots and disturbances. Collecting intelligence data should be a day-to-day operation, with staff from every part of the institution and every level of the organization involved.

Inmates also are a good source of intelligence, if the information they provide is used responsibly and properly corroborated. Experience has shown that staff can collect more and better information from respected inmates (Gettinger 1980) than from dubious informants, who are willing to trade information for privileges and special favors. Undue reliance on this type of information can lead to a narrowly based intelligence system that reflects the informants' manipulative tendencies and personal interests.

It can also create a "paranoid" institutional climate, in which every inmate is "watching his back" and tensions are higher than necessary. Labeled "snitches," such inmates often become the target of great hostility from other inmates. As the New Mexico riot (in which numerous inmate informers were murdered by other inmates) indicated, such a narrowly based system of intelligence can have disastrous effects.

Information gathering should be systematized, not haphazard. Most institutions of any size should have a formal investigative capacity in the form of a dedicated position filled by a supervisory staff member (usually a member of the security force). This person's sole responsibility is to manage the investigative and intelligence functions.

This person should serve as the collection point for all intelligence gathering in the institution, maintain up-to-date records, and collate all intelligence. In addition, this person should be responsible for maintaining nickname files, "posted picture" files used to educate staff about special problem inmates, as well as files on ringleaders in past plots, gang leaders, racists, and drug dealers. This person in most cases also serves as the institution's prime liaison with outside law enforcement officials in coordinating criminal investigative activity in the institution.

Finally, top staff should be briefed daily on the status of the institution by those who have access to this information. An end-of-the-day closeout, where the warden meets with top staff, has been found to be an effective device for this information exchange. It also is the time to plan for the evening's or next day's response to any troubling conditions that may have been identified. Other weekly department head and department-level meetings can be used to good effect as well.

HANDLING GRIEVANCES

Prompt and specific handling of inmates' complaints and grievances is essential in maintaining good morale. A firm "no" answer can be as effective as granting a request in reducing an individual inmate's tensions. This is particularly true if the individual feels the appropriate officials have genuinely considered his problem, and if the inmate is given a reason for the denial. Equivocation and vague answers create false hopes and thus increase the inmate's anger when nothing is done.

A formal grievance procedure is essential in preventing grievances from becoming sources of disorder. A procedure such as that promulgated by the Civil Rights of Institutionalized Persons Act of 1980 is a functional solution to this problem. The grievance procedure should include, at a minimum, the elements set forth in ACA Standard 2-4268 in the *Standards for Adult Correctional Institutions, Second Edition* (1981).

A dangerous situation can arise, however, when inmates have grievances they feel can be corrected only if the proper officials are made aware of their problems, but they have no avenues available to them to voice those concerns. A similar problem exists when an institution has a grievance system that inmates have no confidence in. Inmates know that disturbances are certain to give their complaints wide publicity when less drastic measures fail.

There are some significant grievances that institution staff can do little or nothing about. These usually involve an inmate's original

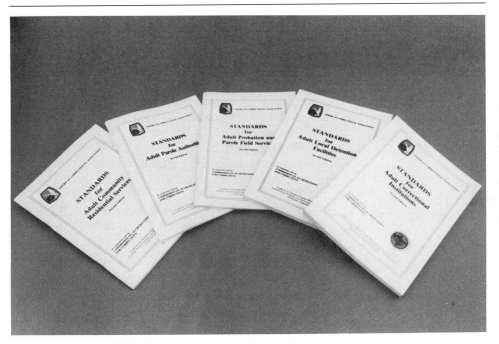

conviction, or the manner in which the paroling authority has handled a specific decision. The institutional staff can explain policies, have representatives of the paroling authority do so, or inform inmates of the proper appeal channels.

This is another area illustrated in the Oakdale/Atlanta disturbances. The Cuban detainees clearly expressed their dissatisfaction with INS procedures and treatment they had received from INS staff. If INS staff had been in the institutions, and if they had sufficient credibility with the detainee population to allay their fears about repatriation to Cuba, the uprising could have been prevented, or at least restricted to a smaller number of participants.

POLICY ISSUES

Correctional supervisors should ensure that all staff under their supervision are following the policies established by the institution. One significant cause of prison disturbances can be the breakdown of organizational procedures, either because of lax supervision or poor training, combined with staff indifference or complacency.

Written policy and procedures, providing a rationale for administrative decisions, are additional preventive tools. All policies and procedures relating to inmate behavior should be made available to inmates during orientation to the institution and in the inmate library. Staff should receive comparable information during pre-service and refresher training.

Administrators must ensure that equitable practices are used in managing inmates, and they must pay particular attention to areas of basic concern to all inmates. Palatable food, adequate clothing, good sanitation and medical care, access to telephones and visiting, prompt mail service, and fair assignment practices must be provided in a manner that a reasonable person can accept.

However, what is regarded as a reasonable administrative decision is subject to change in a time of rising inmate expectations and court intervention, and managers must be flexible enough to adapt to change in critical social and legal perspectives. Relatively broad access to courts and lawyers, and the right to prepare legal appeals, for example, are basic legal rights today that were considered exceptional just a few decades ago. On the other hand, a public shift toward a more punitive correctional philosophy cannot be overlooked entirely, or the agency will suffer a credibility problem. The proper balance here is a vital internal management concern.

STANDARDS AND ACCREDITATION

ACA's standards and accreditation process can provide a comprehensive framework for general riot prevention. A great deal of progress has been made in many areas of corrections in recent years, and most leaders in the field have reached the point of willingness to acknowledge long-standing problems and seek appropriate solutions. In this process, corrections has adopted national standards that address minimum conditions and standardized levels of performance for correctional facilities. The American Correctional Association and the

Commission on Accreditation for Corrections have gathered, refined, and published these standards, which were first published in 1977 and have been repeatedly reviewed, revised, and upgraded. A second edition of *Standards for Adult Correctional Institutions* was published in April 1981, and a third edition is expected to be issued in January 1990. Hundreds of institutions at the federal, state, and local levels have been accredited.

The adoption of uniform national standards and their use in accreditation are positive steps correctional professionals can take to eliminate many of the causes of riots and disturbances, as well as to remedy other adverse, unprofessional conditions in institutions. However, in even the best-managed, accredited facilities, problems can arise. The human factor in corrections is

Prompt and specific handling of inmates' complaints and grievances is essential in maintaining good morale.

inescapable—a single inmate can spark a small incident into a major conflict just as easily as an inexperienced staff member can fan the flames of inmate unrest.

5

Prevention-Related
Security Issues

Every activity and function in an institution must operate within a conscious security policy. Regrettably, the evolution of participatory management, expanded public access, and inmate councils (in a small number of institutions) have incorrectly led to the belief that security is no longer the top priority in many correctional institutions. To take this position is to commit a fundamental error—basic security practices are still the backbone of any institution's safe, secure operation.

PHYSICAL PLANT DESIGN

An important aspect of security is the institution's physical design, particularly in maximum- and medium-security facilities and jails. To contain the inmate population in these institutions, a sound, secure perimeter, featuring guard towers or mobile patrols, double fences, and appropriate alarm systems and lighting, is essential. These features, along with proper fence separation, keeping buildings away from the perimeter, and other features of a well-defined perimeter prevent escapes. They also provide assurance to the community that it is being protected, and keep intruders from accessing the facility grounds.

To enhance perimeter security and the effectiveness of the staff manning it, the perimeter should have a complete electronic detection system, and a telecommunications system between perimeter posts and the institution's control center. Fence construction should include proper separation between fences and between

the fences and all structures and a clear line of sight between perimeter posts.

The internal layout of a correctional facility can also contribute to or greatly hamper security and control. Blind alleys and corners, large, multitiered cellhouses, and architectural designs that separate staff and inmates reduce the level of supervision and diminish control in a prison. Design features that open up the interior to visual supervision, while still permitting quick segmentation during a crisis, are preferred.

Also increasingly preferred are designs that place staff in direct contact with inmates in housing units. While closed-circuit television or even unit control centers may be desirable to supplement direct staff supervision, it is becoming evident that direct supervision patterns are superior in most correctional settings. They allow not only improved communications and observation of inmate behavior patterns, but facilitate security inspections, room searches, and other important security procedures.

An institution's size can also play an important part in establishing control. The ACA standards reflect institutions with 500-bed units as an ideal, in terms of providing administrative span of control and delivery of inmate services. This size institution, or a larger institution partitioned so that 500 or fewer inmates are in each administrative component, can facilitate communications, simplify program and security control, and thus decrease the likelihood of a disturbance. Within the 500-bed unit, smaller organizational or functional units, based on housing areas, can help managers convey and

disseminate rules, regulations, and general information much more quickly with less chance of rumors adversely affecting operations.

There are other important interior design factors. Adequate facilities should be available for storing records, drugs, combustible materials, and other implements that are vital to an institution's operation but have security implications. Weapon and key storage areas should be outside the institution's secure perimeter or in a totally secure control center not susceptible to inmate takeover. The control center itself must be secure enough to withstand a 30- to 45-minute period of attack, to give response staff time to muster their resources in a major disturbance and to drive rioting inmates away from the area.

In determining the locations of critical supplies, electrical vaults and emergency generators, utility cut-offs, and other key operational areas, administrators must envision the possibility of a complete takeover and the implications for retaking the facility of loss of those areas to rioters. Tunnels, sallyports, and other access points should be secure, foreclosing all of these avenues as escape options and reducing the likelihood of a minor disturbance spreading.

Maintaining all utilities and communications systems in operating order is most important under normal conditions, and extremely vital in the event of a riot. Although it is desirable that every institution have two distinctly separate electrical service systems, this might prove prohibitively expensive. Nevertheless, critical electrical systems in the control center and on the perimeter must be backed up by an emergency power system. Several emergency generators at remote locations and in different zones are more desirable from a security standpoint. Emergency electric power to the central control room and the hospital are mandatory.

It is important to emphasize that the physical features of an institution's perimeter, by themselves, are useless without staff properly trained to be alert to their responsibilities while

Design features that open the interior to visual supervision, while still permitting quick segmentation during a crisis, are preferred.

operating a post. Weapons qualifications, training in emergency response policies, and a clear understanding of the agency hostage policy are critical to any staff on the perimeter.

CLASSIFICATION

A well-designed classification system contributes to an efficiently managed correctional program by pooling all of the relevant information concerning the inmate. Inmate classification and reclassification, coupled with proper institutional placement, are important security factors—perhaps as important as the security provided by bricks and mortar.

Proper classification also provides the opportunity to structure the institution's population to minimize the likelihood of a riot or disturbance. In recent years, inmate classification has resulted in the identification of special inmate groups requiring unusual security or housing. Included in these categories are protective custody cases, unusually high security cases, and violent, predatory inmates (including prison gang members) who require confinement in long-term special management units. In setting up such units, administrators will reap the benefits of removing a number of the potential sources of disruption leading to riots or disturbances. The

classification system should not be automatic. It should allow for staff to override any numerical or mechanical determinations that, in their best professional judgment, are not appropriate. Reclassification procedures should allow for necessary decreases and increases in custody without the burden of due process.

The first decision that should be made with classification information is what level of security the inmate requires. In general, the principal purpose of classification should be to place each inmate in the least restrictive setting consistent with the protection of society, staff, and other inmates. Once that important determination is complete, then a program can be devised that is realistically in line with the individual's needs and the resources of the specific institution, all within the necessary bounds of security.

After the institutional assignment is made on the basis of security considerations, programs or classification options should be made available to meet the needs of inmates at each security level. This suggests that a number of options should exist in each institution.

Furthermore, by dividing the inmate population into smaller groups on some rational classification basis, the likelihood of a major disturbance is greatly reduced. If a unit management concept is used, communication is enhanced because staff become responsible for fewer inmates and more staff become involved in the classification process. Having a variety of different groups or classifications also aids in another important classification function— separating or isolating the troublemakers.

One useful outcome of the classification process has been the inception of special management or control units for dangerous or predatory inmates. These units are relatively small and require unusually strong physical controls as well as carefully designed procedural safeguards for staff. However, these programs have received increasingly close court scrutiny in recent years.

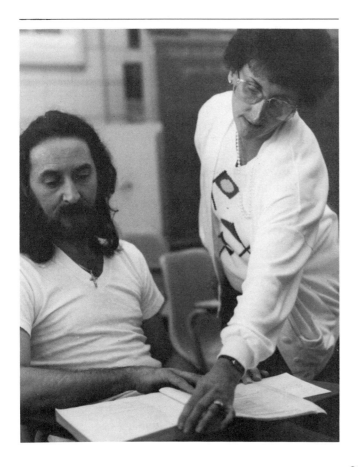

Not only are program staff

increasingly seen as

important employees, but the

security value of their

activities is now well

recognized.

All people—staff included—

who move into and out of the

institution must be considered

possible avenues of

contraband movement.

Careful attention must be paid to establishing rational criteria for selection, regular review procedures for release, and sound, legally defensible operating procedures. The unit's underlying policy and philosophy must properly balance legitimate inmate rights in certain fundamental areas against the institution's equally important security needs. Under those circumstances, such units can serve as a major preventive factor for institutional disruptions.

TOOL CONTROL

Virtually every item in an institution can be considered a potential weapon. However, staff cannot control every item; they must focus their efforts on those materials and tools that clearly have the greatest potential for weapon or contraband use or contraband fabrication.

In any major institution there are thousands of tools necessary for the functioning of maintenance shops, the food service department, industries, and vocational education areas. To effectively limit the improper use of these items, it is mandatory to maintain a system of tool control.

Each institution must develop an effective tool control system that is easily understood by staff. Division of tools into categories according to potential weapon or escape use is a key element in most tool control plans. Shadow boards and tool checkout systems are functional and easy to place into effect. Periodic inventories of all equipment and tools are a must. Again, no control system can function adequately without the staff's sensitivity to the institution's security, or without providing the necessary training in the program and supervision of its implementation.

Industrial and maintenance areas are prime sources of both dangerous tools and materials that may be used as or made into weapons. While it is particularly difficult to maintain constant supervision of these areas and the assigned workers, effective search procedures for all inmates leaving the area are essential. Inmates who leave on pass during the regular working shift should be searched carefully.

Care should be taken to avoid the tendency to routinize the security procedures and provide searches only at shift end. A screening type of security for tool control can be achieved by developing search procedures at the point where the inmates enter the general housing area, using a combination of pat searches and hand-held or walk-through metal detectors.

CONTRABAND CONTROL

Each institution defines contraband somewhat differently, usually as a result of past experience and values peculiar to that institution. Contraband is generally considered to be items such as weapons, drugs, or printed information the administration feels may negatively affect the prison's operation or security. A somewhat broader definition includes any item not issued by the institution or authorized by staff for receipt or retention from outside the institution, or any otherwise approved item that has been modified in an impermissible manner.

All people—staff included—who move into and out of the institution must be considered possible avenues of contraband movement. For that reason, it is necessary to have well-defined search procedures for all people and items entering and leaving the institution. This should not, however, be interpreted as leading to routine searches of all staff.

Materials that are not contraband in one area of the institution may be considered contraband

in another. Knives from the kitchen or paint thinner from the paint shop are only two examples of the kinds of materials that would be considered contraband if found in cells. Issue clothing modified to resemble an officer's uniform is an example of how otherwise permissible items can become contraband.

KEY CONTROL

Key control is an absolutely indispensable part of any institution's security system. Each key and key ring in the institution must be positively identified and accounted for at all times. A positive key issue system must be devised for each specific institution, as well as a method for accounting for every key in the institution every day.

This means that a secure storage area must be available for issue, spare, and pattern keys, a well-defined and maintained inventory system has to be in place, and issue procedures must be carefully enforced. A system for maintaining and issuing restricted keys to critical areas also must be developed and enforced. Staff must be trained in the system, and in sound key-handling procedures.

Staff should also be thoroughly trained in the use of emergency keys, to facilitate access to any part of the institution in an emergency. This system in particular is vital in the successful implementation of any riot plan.

BODY SEARCHES

Inmates can and do conceal contraband on their person, either in clothing or on their body. For that reason, staff must be trained in proper search techniques, using methods approved by the agency.

Pat searches of an inmate's clothing and outer body can be done at any time, and are a useful preventive and detection device in suppressing contraband.

Unless it is an emergency, body or "strip" searches should take place in a private area, such as in a room, booth, or behind a curtain. A body cavity search only takes place if there is a reasonable belief that the inmate is carrying contraband.

Inspection of body cavities such as the nasal cavities, rectum, or vagina, whether manually or by instrument, should only be conducted with good cause, and when authorized by the warden or designee. Searches of this type must be conducted in private, by health care personnel or other staff who have been specifically trained in these procedures.

When officers search a large group of inmates, such as a work detail, they should order the inmates to line up and present themselves one at a time for search. The first person searched then forms the start of a new line far enough from the unsearched people to prevent the passing of contraband. After the searches are complete, the officer should scan the area where inmates stood to locate any contraband that may have been dropped or discarded.

AREA SEARCHES

Area searches are a necessary part of the life of any institution and its inmates; they are an important procedure for protecting inmates and staff. They are a primary means of discouraging the collection or fabrication of contraband and the detection of breaches that could lead to disruptions or escapes.

Staff should conduct routine and special searches of school, work, and industrial areas, as well as living areas. Searches of this type need not be confined to security personnel, but should be conducted on a frequent but irregular basis by the staff who work in the area itself. Logs should be kept of the searches, noting the areas searched, items found, and their disposition.

The methods employed in searches—their timing, excessive use, or destruction of inmate property—are often cause for inmate grievances, disturbances, or litigation. The most serious complaint, and the most common finding of courts in regard to searches, is that they have been used on occasion as a means of harassing inmates. Everyone living or working in an institution knows that searches are necessary. Search procedures are not generally questioned if they are accomplished in a professional manner, and reflect consideration of inmates' legitimate property rights. Thoroughness is important, but so is following the institution's rules with regard to professional search techniques.

SECURITY INSPECTIONS

Every institution should have a well-developed system that ensures that all physical security features are checked on a regular basis. Such a system includes specific staff assignments to inspection of specific areas on a specific timetable. It also should entail completing a required inspection form, which is turned in to a supervisory staff member for accountability and follow-up.

Staff performing security inspections must ensure, in addition to typical physical security checks on doors, bars, locks, etc., that doors and locks are not painted shut, that ice and snow are cleared from exits in the winter, and that items are not stored in passageways and access corridors. Hand in hand with these inspections there should be a regular program for testing all emergency keys and the locks to the emergency doors, so there is no question about quick access in a crisis.

EFFECTIVE COMMUNICATION SYSTEMS

Technological communications play an important part in preventing and responding to crises. The effective use of radios, intercoms, and other devices certainly is an important part of contemporary institutional operations. Institutional messages recorded on dedicated telephone lines, or through relatively simple computer-based systems, can be excellent for keeping staff updated on institutional events, policy changes, and other facts.

Personal body alarms are particularly valuable communications devices. They enable a disabled staff member, or one who has witnessed a serious incident, to quickly and unobtrusively signal a problem to a remote staff member, usually in the control center. This allows a prompt response, which is not only in the interest of the employee's personal safety, but also can result in quelling a small disturbance before it gets out of hand.

INMATE PROGRAMS

One common misconception held by some staff is that programs are incompatible with security. This belief is probably traceable to a past day in corrections when programs operated in isolation and were provided by staff who were not fully integrated into the institution's operation. This is becoming less and less the case; not only are program staff increasingly seen as important employees, but the security value of their activities is now well recognized.

First of all, programs provide constructive time structuring for inmates, under direct staff supervision. When inmates are in school, on the recreation yard, or in a vocational training class, they are not loitering in quarters, where correctional officer coverage is typically low. Time spent in good programs is time that inmates are not able to actively plot escapes, drug trafficking, or other illegal activities.

A wide range of institutional programs and activities can have a positive effect on morale, in addition to helping inmates prepare for their return to society. Most administrators believe that when inmates have a wide choice of self-improvement activities or constructive leisure programs, tensions are reduced and the individual inmate is less inclined toward disruptive behavior.

Formal, budgeted programs such as education should be organized according to accepted professional guidelines. Inmate volunteer groups should be regulated by a policy that includes a requirement for submitting a statement of purpose, rules or procedures, and meeting times, etc., with all group activities under the direct supervision of a staff member. Appropriate administrative controls and staff supervision will prevent use of the group as a power base by predatory inmates or for the planning of disruptive activities.

Where citizens from the community wish to help in an activity, they should be carefully supervised and informed, through an orientation, about the nature of the correctional environment. This orientation should also cover limits they must observe in personal conduct in the institution and in their relationships with inmates.

6

Planning for Disturbance Control

Institutional disturbances may range from a small flare-up among several inmates to a major riot involving a large portion of the population, from a passive "sit-down" demonstration in the yard to large-scale, random, senseless destruction of life and property. Disturbances may arise from spontaneous reactions to some critical incident such as a stabbing. They may be organized, calculated movements of massive resistance, supported and assisted by outside groups and led by intelligent inmates using revolutionary tactics. They may be an attempt to salvage a failed escape attempt. In short, each is distinctly different.

As a result, each type of disturbance also requires distinctly different response and control tactics. Therefore, it is essential that any master riot plan be sufficiently flexible so that the response can be tailored to each individual situation.

EMERGENCY PLANS

Once under way, controlling a riot or disturbance is one of the most difficult tasks a correctional administrator can face. It is, therefore, imperative to develop a response plan and determine in advance how to organize resources that can be put into action on very short notice.

A well-written riot control plan provides administrators with sufficient response flexibility, and is clearly and concisely written so that it is easily understood by all. It ensures deployment of all personnel and equipment to the problem areas as quickly and efficiently as possible. A sample emergency plan is contained in Appendix E.

A well-developed plan will have basic content on the following elements.

Prevention and Signs of Tension

The plan should contain information on the prevention of riots and detection of signs of tension, as outlined earlier in this publication.

Reporting Incidents

The emergency plan should emphasize the need to report a disturbance immediately to a central location, usually the control center. This allows officials maximum time to isolate and bring the problem under control before it escalates and involves a greater area or more inmates.

Chain of Command

The plan should clearly set forth the chain of command for both the interim response (until regular command staff arrive) and long-term tactical and strategic command activity, including hostage negotiations. As soon as the chief executive officer of the institution arrives on location, he or she should assume command, with associate or deputy-level managers responsible for functions that are clearly delineated in the emergency plan.

Notification and Call-up Procedures

Upon being notified of a disturbance, the control center officer should contact the shift

> *It is essential that any master riot plan be sufficiently flexible so that the response can be tailored to each individual situation.*

supervisor. The plan should then specify prompt notification of staff on perimeter posts, front and rear entrances, the powerhouse, all areas where there are likely to be groups of inmates, and then administrative staff—the warden, associate warden, chief correctional supervisor, and others. If the shift supervisor cannot be contacted, the control center officer ordinarily is authorized to initiate these emergency notification procedures independently.

Command Center Operations

The plan should identify the location of a command center in a totally secure area of the institution. An auxiliary command center should also be identified outside the secure compound, so that in the unlikely event the prime command center is overrun by inmates, tactical and strategic activity can still be coordinated from a functional location with communications and other capabilities.

Intelligence Gathering

The plan should address the need to gather as quickly as possible information about the nature and scope of the disturbance, number of staff hostages (if any), and other key facts. If the situation continues, then an ongoing intelligence-gathering and analysis process must be in place.

Selection and Assignment of Emergency Squads

The plan should clearly identify the categories of staff to be mustered for response action, how they are to be organized, and timekeeping and other administrative details. The plan should specify where squads will be staged while awaiting action.

Notification of Outside Parties

Specific authority to notify local law enforcement authorities should be contained in the plan; local utility companies may also have to be notified to help staff maintain or cut off utility service in the institution.

Use of Outside Assistance

The plan should describe staff deployment methods and provide that only trained correctional officers are assigned inside an institution during a disturbance, unless the situation is so serious as to require the police or National Guard to provide additional coverage in retaking the facility. Outside law enforcement personnel and institutional staff who are untrained in riot control may be used to secure the perimeter, to control gates, or to supervise areas where they are unlikely to encounter inmates.

Developing Options for Action

The riot plan should contain general information on the tactical options available for retaking the institution, from securing a single, small area to arranging an assault to retake the entire compound.

While each crisis differs, there is no doubt that similar principles can be employed in many riot situations. The plan should contain information on squad use, deployment of gas, utility controls, and other crowd and riot suppression activities. It also should include an awareness of the importance of a measured, professional, nonpunitive response to small-scale incidents, so as to avoid alienating the majority of inmates, who may not be active participants, as is often the case. These nonparticipants should be moved as soon as possible to pre-identified, fenced areas close to towers, or to well-supervised buildings suitable for this purpose. Inmates can be secured in these areas without risk of causing further disruption, fed, showered, and even offered recreational activities—all under appropriate supervision—throughout the duration of the disturbance.

Selection and Use of Equipment

The plan should provide for rapid issue of emergency equipment to staff only, including items such as riot helmets, batons, communication equipment, shotguns, gas and gas equipment, shields, emergency keys, cutting torches, large bolt cutters, wrenches, wrecking bars, ropes, and portable lights. This often is done by maintaining ready boxes of enough personal equipment to outfit one squad, and pre-prepared weapons kits that have a firearm, ammunition, and other necessary gear ready for issue from the armory.

Weapon and Equipment Accountability

All equipment issued must be accounted for through a pre-prepared, positive identification system of some type. The confusion of a riot is no time to try to set up an accountability system.

Follow-up

The riot plan must address not only the actual emergency and the retaking of the institution from a tactical point of view. It must at least consider the post-riot considerations noted later in this publication.

A riot control plan cannot be centrally dictated or compiled by a parent agency. Instead, it must be carefully developed by the staff of each institution, who can tailor it to the facility's unique needs and characteristics. The plan must provide administrators with sufficient response

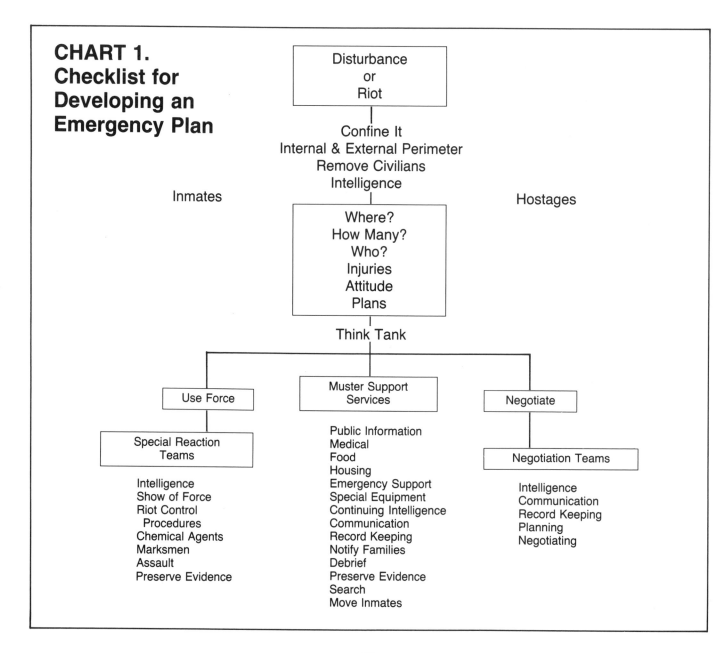

CHART 1. Checklist for Developing an Emergency Plan

Disturbance or Riot

Confine It
Internal & External Perimeter
Remove Civilians
Intelligence

Inmates

Where?
How Many?
Who?
Injuries
Attitude
Plans

Hostages

Think Tank

Use Force

Muster Support Services

Negotiate

Special Reaction Teams

Intelligence
Show of Force
Riot Control
 Procedures
Chemical Agents
Marksmen
Assault
Preserve Evidence

Public Information
Medical
Food
Housing
Emergency Support
Special Equipment
Continuing Intelligence
Communication
Record Keeping
Notify Families
Debrief
Preserve Evidence
Search
Move Inmates

Negotiation Teams

Intelligence
Communication
Record Keeping
Planning
Negotiating

It is imperative to determine in advance how to organize resources that can be put into action on very short notice.

flexibility and must also be developed in a clear and concise style that is easily understood. The plan's objective should be to provide for rapid crisis assessment and rapid, efficient deployment of all necessary response resources into the problem area. A plan that successfully accomplishes this will minimize injury, death, and damage by denying rioters time to organize and consolidate.

Some of the alternatives and tasks that need to be considered are shown in Chart 1, which may serve as a checklist in developing an emergency plan for a specific institution. Appendix E provides a sample riot control plan and further details.

Once a disturbance breaks out, a riot plan, per se, has little value unless line supervisors and staff have been trained in its activation. Segments of the disturbance plan, including use of gas and other emergency equipment, should be simulated during pre-employment and annual refresher training sessions.

POST ORDERS

In connection with riot plan content, concise post orders must be maintained on all posts throughout the institution, outlining the specific functions of each post within the overall plan. Certain posts, such as the armory, perimeter gates, and the control center, should have highly detailed descriptive information on the procedures necessary in a disturbance. Gate identification processes, weapon issue, and many other typical activities will change dramatically in a disturbance, and post orders should spell out these changes.

For instance, in the control center or other location where keys are issued, it should be clearly stated in the post orders that some sets of keys that are routinely drawn by certain employees will be restricted during such emergencies. These would include keys to knife cabinets, the central tool room, armory, narcotic storage areas, and administrative offices. The control center officer should attempt to recall keys to certain critical areas like the tool rooms

and narcotic storage areas, if time permits.

The riot plan and post orders must be treated confidentially; they should not be available to the general public or accessible to the inmate population. Agency freedom of information procedures should specify that the emergency plans cannot be released. However, even though confidential, they should not be kept from staff. Every staff member must review the plan at least annually, and this should be done through a formal checkout procedure, or in a restricted, non-inmate contact area of the institution.

When emergency plans are developed, it should be remembered that they are, in essence, training plans also. Staff training centers and training officers should have the emergency plan information, and use it to develop training programs that include hypothetical situations and even dramatization of some events, like hostage situations. The emergency plans also should be used to develop the audit format and guidelines that the agency uses to evaluate institutional effectiveness.

CHART 2.
Organizational Chart for Riot Situations*

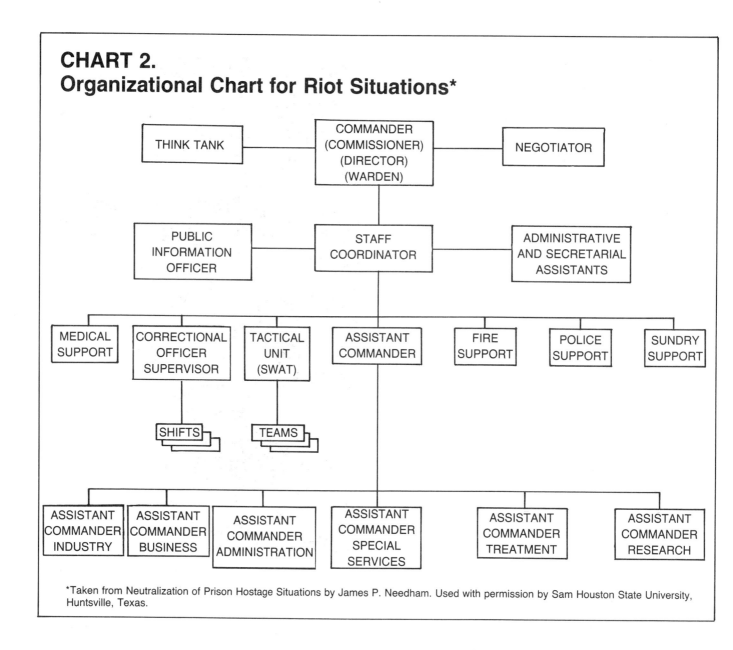

*Taken from Neutralization of Prison Hostage Situations by James P. Needham. Used with permission by Sam Houston State University, Huntsville, Texas.

ORGANIZATION OF THE RESPONSE

The plan should specify one person who is in charge of the entire response situation. Typically, this would be the warden of the institution. It is also important that other institutional staff roles during disturbances are identified in an organizational chart, which clearly shows the chain of command. Chart 2 shows a typical organizational configuration.

As part of planning for riot control, there should be agreement on the roles of the governor, attorney general, county attorney, state police commander, National Guard commander, and other officials. The agency's headquarters office and the heads of each institution must ensure that such understandings exist. If possible, these agreements should be in writing, with responsible persons and contact points identified in the emergency plan.

PREMISES FOR RIOT CONTROL

All parties and agencies involved in responding to a riot should agree on certain fundamental premises. The following are strongly recommended for adoption as part of the riot plan and any formal interagency agreements that may be in effect:

- Rioters will be granted no illegal freedom.
- Neither immunity nor amnesty will be granted.
- Prosecution will be sought wherever possible.
- A person under duress, such as a hostage, has no authority and loses all status.

■ Neither keys nor weapons will be surrendered.

■ Neither drugs nor liquor will be provided.

■ No transportation will be provided to help inmates leave the institution.

MOBILIZING STAFF AND OTHER RESOURCES

In the plan, the mobilization of personnel should be described generally in four phases:

1. Mobilization of on-duty personnel
2. Call-up of off-duty personnel
3. Mobilization of other agency personnel
4. If deemed necessary by the warden, the mobilization of support personnel from law enforcement agencies and/or the National Guard

This ranking reflects the principle that only trained institutional personnel should be assigned inside an institution during a disturbance, unless a situation is so totally out of control that police or the National Guard must be involved. Once agency staff have been deployed, if additional manpower resources are needed, then law enforcement personnel can appropriately be used for perimeter security, gate control, or any other areas where they will not be in direct contact with the inmates.

Any staff with qualifications for specific weapons or equipment should be clearly identified in the plan. But because of the highly specialized training involved, it is recommended that consideration be given to forming a special response team in larger institutions. These employees are highly qualified in not only special weapons use, but other response tactics as well.

Enough staff should be identified and trained at this higher skill level to minimize the shortfalls associated with shift work, vacations, and job turnover. Careful records should be kept on those who receive such training so they can be identified and located quickly. Members of special teams of this type may be issued pagers so they can be quickly recalled to a central muster point in the institution, or even from off-duty locations.

It is important to note that these special teams should not be considered a complete replacement for other staff response options. Most institutions train all security staff in squad formations and tactics, and some systems train all staff for this purpose. Special response teams are best regarded as a carefully selected supplementary force, to be used to help the other squad-type groups composed of regular staff.

PHYSICAL PLANT ISSUES IN DISTURBANCES

Once beyond basic architecture and design and modifications desirable for making buildings more secure, the riot control plan should begin with an analysis of all facilities and utility systems. The administration must have a complete knowledge of both the visible and concealed features of the institution.

To supplement the personal familiarity of top staff with the institution, a complete set of plans for the institution and all of its buildings and utilities should be used in drafting the riot plan and also should be available during any crisis. These plans should be stored in a secure but readily available area outside the inmate compound. They should not be as-built drawings, but must reflect all modifications made in the institution, so that staff are briefed on plans that are current and accurate. The best possible response plans can go awry if a grille door or a second security lock has been installed, and no one recalls that change in the heat of the moment.

KEEPING THE PLAN UPDATED

After developing a plan for dealing with disturbances, it is essential to follow up with frequent inspections to ensure that equipment is in good order. Procedures must be reviewed at least annually to ensure that they are still functional.

A checklist for periodic review of the plan should include but not necessarily be limited to the following areas:

- Inventory and inspection of all firearms and ammunition to keep them updated
- Inventory and inspection of the gas supply and equipment, so that the gas supply can be updated and old gas may be used for training purposes
- Tests of emergency lighting equipment and facilities, including those available from outside agencies
- Inspections of fire-fighting equipment
- Regular confirmation and logging of the location and operability of shut-off valves for water, electricity, gas, heat, and ventilation
- Tests of the operability of all emergency entrances to all buildings

EMERGENCY EQUIPMENT

A comprehensive and detailed list of all weapons, tools, and equipment that might be required in the control of a major crisis situation is beyond the scope of this publication. Some general categories can be mentioned, however.

Special equipment should be maintained in constant readiness, reserved for emergency use only. It should include such items as riot helmets, jumpsuits, batons, bullhorns, shotguns, gas and gas equipment, shields, emergency keys, cutting torches, wrenches, wrecking bars, ladders, ropes, and portable lights. These items should be stored in the armory or other totally secure area outside the confines of the institution proper, like a tower. When possible, protective clothing and other individual equipment items should be pre-boxed in containers with squad-sized quantities, which can be moved quickly to a mustering area for issue. Weapons, ammunition, and gas equipment should be issued directly from the armory, with proper accountability procedures to ensure the return of all items at the end of the disturbance.

Barricade removal may require the use of axes, crowbars, pinch bars, and other tools. There may also be a need for special concrete- and steel-cutting equipment to gain access to buildings or to allow inmates who do not want to participate in the disturbance a chance to exit. Night vision scopes may be extremely useful at times, if only to provide intelligence information to command staff on the location of hostages or other key inmate activities.

After developing a plan for dealing with disturbances, it is essential to follow up with frequent inspections to ensure that equipment is in good order.

■ Tests of the emergency key system and rotation of keys

■ Tests of the general alarm system—siren, radios, pagers, etc.

■ Periodic familiarization of all fire response personnel (including those from the local community) with the plan itself, and with the procedures for mustering the institutional fire crews

■ Reviews of the availability of emergency personnel: current telephone lists and regular review of staff recall procedures themselves, which may use sequential calls, sirens, computer call-up systems, or other methods

■ Tests of amplifiers, public address systems, and communication equipment

■ Reviews of the location of critical and hazardous supplies, especially those that can be burned or used as weapons, i.e., gasoline, poisons, ladders, torches, etc.

Use of Force

7

Sometimes use of force is necessary to quell a riot or prevent it from spreading. For example, negotiations may fail or those in charge may judge other factors and recommend the use of force. At times, the show of superior force might be enough to convince rioters to surrender. A display of trained staff with riot control gear has proved effective in bringing some disturbances to a prompt conclusion. However, if this is not enough, then direct force must be used. In those cases, the most common strategy is to deploy multiple squad-type formations and use smoke, water hoses, or chemical agents to confuse or temporarily disable rioters. Squad formations thus become an important part of the application of force in such situations.

SQUAD FORMATIONS

The five most common riot control formations are: (1) "the line," used to move a group of rioters directly away (e.g., down a corridor); (2) "echelon right," used to move a group of rioters to the left; (3) "echelon left," used to move a group of rioters to the right; (4) "the wedge," used to disperse rioters to either side; and (5) "the diamond," used to provide protection on all sides.

For psychological purposes in the institution, it may prove advantageous to deploy squad formations with staff equipped with riot batons, interspersed with others armed with shotguns. Use of deadly force should be avoided unless other methods have failed or it becomes necessary to save lives and prevent serious injury, property damage, or escapes.

Any use of deadly force must be clearly in line with agency policy and state statutes that regulate such actions. Staff must be thoroughly familiar

with the constraints imposed by these regulations, and clearly established rules of engagement must be set forth before the rioters are confronted. If the situation requires using deadly force, it should be employed with utmost precision and selectivity against the particular threat that justifies its use. When possible, its use should be preceded by a clear warning that the use of such force is contemplated. An important consideration here is to balance the tactical advantages against the potential risk to the hostages that might occur if the inmates have time to prepare for an actual assault.

Staff who have been issued firearms must be given direct orders regarding the rules of engagement for the use of deadly force; they must know and abide by specific agency policy in using deadly force. In general, firearms should be used only when other means fail, and then only if less extreme measures will not serve the same purpose. In most jurisdictions, an officer may fire under the following circumstances:

■ At an inmate or other person carrying a weapon or attempting to obtain a weapon in order to harm others
■ At an inmate or other person the officer sees kill or seriously injure any person (whether or not a weapon is used) and who refuses to halt when ordered
■ At an escaping inmate who cannot be stopped by nonlethal measures
■ To protect fire-fighting equipment or vital property
■ To contain inmates to prevent the disturbance from spreading to other zones

Using deadly force always entails considerable risks, and everything possible should be done to

minimize them. The following are some suggestions:

■ Those entrusted with firearms should be highly trained and carefully screened, to ensure that they are not "trigger happy."

■ Marksmen should have a particular weapon assigned to them that they are familiar with and that they have personally zeroed.

■ All firearms and loads should be carefully allocated so they are appropriate for the purpose and setting in which they may be used.

■ Those using weapons should aim to disable rather than kill.

■ All who participate in an assault should be carefully briefed as to what they are likely to encounter; they should know the building and the location of the rioters.

■ If hostages are involved, their identity and locations are critical; all those involved must be aware of the possibility that inmates might have forced hostages to exchange clothes, thus making identification more difficult.

■ Those participating in the assault should be properly equipped. Protective gear such as "flak jackets" or vests should be worn, as should helmets and boots.

■ If the use of chemical agents is anticipated, gas masks should be available.

If the situation requires using deadly force, it should be employed with utmost precision and selectivity.

RIOT CONTROL WEAPONS AND EQUIPMENT

Specialized weapons and equipment can be invaluable in quelling a riot. As part of general riot preparedness, most facilities have some or all of the following equipment items available.

Protective Equipment

Staff assigned to the riot area should be provided with protective clothing, such as jumpsuits, helmets, shields, gloves, and boots. If the rioters are thought to have weapons, then staff should be provided with body armor. If chemical agents such as tear gas are likely to be employed, then gas masks are mandatory for staff.

43

Squad commanders and control center staff should have gas masks with speaker capability so they can issue necessary orders even if chemical agents are dispersed.

Baton

Perhaps the most frequently used riot control device is the baton. This is an effective weapon in deterring and defending against attack. It is especially useful in close-in situations where a shotgun or pistol would be deadly. Certainly the baton can be lethal, but in the hands of a well-trained officer, it is a very functional protective weapon.

Fire Hoses

Water—especially if delivered from high-pressure fire hoses—can be an effective, nonlethal tool for breaking up groups of inmates, repelling attacking groups, or soaking a group in preparation for the use of gas. Locating fire standpipes, hoses, and other necessary equipment and identifying staff who will be assigned to this task should be a part of the riot control plan.

Firearms

Shotgun

The shotgun is probably the next most common riot control weapon in correctional institutions. In many cases, the intimidation value of such a weapon may render its actual use unnecessary. Twelve-gauge slide-action shotguns are recommended because of their reliability and flexibility. They permit several choices in loads, whereas autoloading shotguns are often limited in the kind of shot rounds they can chamber and reliably cycle in the autoloading action, and most usually cannot use some of the special loads mentioned below.

Selection of a shotshell load is based on the situation to be encountered. Number OO buckshot is less likely to ricochet than a rifle bullet, yet is accurate and offers tremendous stopping power at up to 50 yards. Its use, however, obviously constitutes deadly force. Birdshot (#7½ shot), on the other hand, can provide stopping power without inflicting substantial injury. It is generally recommended that a warning shot be fired initially about three feet in front of rioters so as to ricochet off the floor. This generally proves effective without causing disabling injuries. To avoid serious damage to rioters, the general rule in using the shotgun is to aim low.

A special shotgun shell filled with wooden blocks is also available and has proved effective when used in the same manner as birdshot. Other loads are available and may be considered. These include putty projectiles, soft rubber bullets, tempered glass beads, molded rock salt, and plastic pellets.

> *Firearms should be used only when other means fail, and then only if less extreme measures will not serve the same purpose.*

Stun Devices

The stun gun is another riot control tool. Among the available designs are a special 40 mm hand-held launcher that doubles as a baton and is used to fire a three-inch loading directly at a rioter. It fires a flat, variable diameter shot bag using powder-activated cartridges. It has a nonpenetrating, knockdown effect at various ranges depending on the type of load. Generally the stun gun should not be aimed at the head or neck regions.

A stun bomb has recently been developed for use in aircraft hijacking situations. It is quite expensive, but may be useful in the institutional setting. The bomb is designed not to inflict permanent injury, but the explosion typically disables those exposed to it for several seconds. In some instances, this may provide the time necessary to save a hostage from a precarious situation. Items of this type are useful only when agency staff have had the opportunity to provide proper training, or if special response personnel from another agency with such training have been cleared for rescue activity in the institution.

Rifle

The rifle has no place in crowd or general riot control. However, in the hands of an excellent marksman it may prove very useful in protecting hostages' lives if they are in imminent danger. Specific protective concerns may also justify the use of rifle fire against hostile inmates. Those circumstances might include disabling an inmate attempting to set a building on fire or penetrate the security of a flammable storage area. Telescopic sights are a necessity for accurate rifle fire of this type.

Use of Chemical Agents

Chemical agents can also provide an excellent means of quelling a riot without causing death or severe bodily harm; the most common used in correctional institutions is tear gas. There are two typical varieties: CN (chloracetophenone) and CS (orthochlorobenzalmalononitrile).

CN is the milder form of tear gas, and it is normally used in closed areas. It will cause the skin to smart, irritate the eyes and cause tears, create a burning sensation in the mucous areas, and cause an overall feeling of discomfort. These symptoms are fleeting and will usually disappear within a few minutes after the individual is removed from the contaminated area. People exposed to heavy concentrations for prolonged periods should receive medical attention. General treatment includes using a commercial eyewash or a very diluted salt solution to wash the eyes, and soap and water to wash the body.

CS is more powerful than CN and is sometimes called "super tear gas." It has replaced CN for use by the military. It produces extreme burning of the eyes, coughing, labored breathing, chest tightness, stinging sensations on moist areas of the skin, and nausea. Because of its power, CS requires first aid by knowledgeable personnel. Affected people should be moved to an uncontaminated area, preferably outdoors. They should be cautioned against rubbing their eyes. After three to six hours they should shower with cold water for a few minutes, then shower with soap as usual. CS ordinarily is not to be used indoors because of its potency.

Precautions

Although CS and CN are generally considered nonlethal chemicals, certain precautions should be taken in their use. Medical personnel and equipment should be available. People often panic when exposed to these substances and frequently

Using deadly force always entails considerable risks, and everything possible should be done to minimize them.

injure themselves or others attempting to escape the discomfort. Those with heart or respiratory ailments may have these problems aggravated by tear gas. In extreme concentrations or in enclosed spaces, these chemical agents can prove lethal. Some courts, therefore, consider their use as constituting "deadly force." These factors must be taken into account in deciding whether to use such chemical agents in controlling disturbances. It would also be wise to determine, ahead of time, for each section of a correctional institution, whether gas should be used at all, and if so, in what concentration. This information should be included in the riot plan and the post orders of all posts where gas is maintained.

Alternatives

The use of smoke is a possible alternative to the use of either CN or CS. It may be dispensed in the same manner as tear gas, and may initially produce much the same psychological effect because rioters would probably assume that it is tear gas and seek cover to avoid it.

DM (dephenylaminechlorarsine), commonly referred to as "sickening" or "knock-out" gas, is not recommended for use in correctional institutions. It requires 15 to 30 minutes to take effect and produces increasingly severe nausea. If fully exposed, a person can expect to feel the effects of this gas for up to 24 hours.

All of the chemical agents discussed above are available commercially, and literature concerning them is available from the distributors. They may be dispensed by various means. The most common is a grenade. This can be of the exploding or nonexploding variety, where the agent typically burns and produces smoke. Since the latter varieties have the potential to cause fires, care must be exercised in their deployment.

Another method of dispensing gas is the 37 mm gas gun. There are a variety of cartridges available for this weapon, some of them of the blast dispersion type, where the gas is dispersed in a cloud near the gun; others can go over or penetrate substantial barricades at a distance. Care should be taken not to fire barricade projectiles into the midst of rioters, as they could easily cause serious injury or death.

Chemical agents can also be dispersed mechanically, in the form of a micropulverized powder. The means of dispersing the powder ranges from a small hand-held aerosol can to helicopters, which can cover an entire yard. Another dispensing technique is via a small, lightweight gasoline-powered generator, which vaporizes the gas in a tubular nozzle heated by the engine's exhaust. This is particularly effective in rapid gas deployment in a closed area like a gymnasium or cellhouse. Every close- or maximum-security facility should have a high-volume gas dispenser as part of its emergency equipment.

Actual Disturbance Control

This chapter provides an overview of immediate reaction issues, response issues in long-term crises, media relations, and post-riot activities.

IMMEDIATE REACTION ISSUES

Notification

All staff know how, and to whom, to report a disturbance. Notification should be immediate, and to a central location, usually the control center. A prompt alert will give command officials the maximum amount of time to isolate and bring the disturbance under control before it spreads to a wider area.

Reaction in the Control Center

Upon receiving notification of a disturbance, the control center officer should immediately contact the supervisor in charge of the watch. The control officer's post orders should specify under what circumstances contact should be made with the administrative staff (the warden, associate warden, and chief correctional supervisor). Immediate notification should include, in some predetermined order: perimeter security posts, the entrances, the powerhouse, shop areas, food service, and all other areas where groups of inmates are likely to be. Staff remaining in these areas should be reinforced as soon as possible.

The control center officer receiving an emergency call should ascertain as much as possible about the situation. At a minimum, the following information should be sought:

1. The part of the correctional institution involved

2. The number of inmates involved
3. The number of hostages taken, if any
4. The location of the hostages
5. The identities of the ringleaders

Under many circumstances, however, this amount of detail cannot always be obtained. In the event the control center officer is unable to question the caller, he or she should immediately contact the supervisor of the watch or other available officers to advise them of the emergency call, so they can initiate action to seal off the area where the disturbance is located.

It is at this stage that any immediately available staff should be dispatched to the scene, and any special response staff should be paged or otherwise called to immediate duty. But in addition, each institution should have a means of alerting other staff that an emergency is under way. This may be a whistle, bell system, prearranged telephone signal, pagers, radio, or some other method. This will not only alert staff for their own safety, but also enable them to begin sealing off key zones, locking up tools and hazardous materials, securing inmates, and taking other precautionary actions, even if their area is not involved.

In the event the watch supervisor cannot be contacted or is already involved in the immediate crisis situation, the emergency procedures should allow for the control center officer to institute certain emergency response procedures without further authorization. Therefore, the officers who are assigned to the control center must have extensive experience and knowledge of institutional operations, as well as familiarity with the emergency procedures.

Staff living in government housing areas near

the institution should be warned. The emergency plan should contain provisions for evacuation of housing areas, if necessary. The control center's post orders should also include guidance on notification of outside authorities, such as the fire department and state police, if command staff are unavailable.

Containment

To avoid widespread rioting, the disturbance must be confined to the smallest portion of the institution as soon as possible. When a disturbance occurs, all staff should be alerted and should seal off their areas. As soon as possible thereafter, an internal perimeter should be established to control movement into and out of the location of the disturbance. The external perimeter should be reinforced to control further movement into the institution and to prevent escapes.

The theory of containment is a variation of the "divide and conquer" theory. It is a controlled "lockdown" of all areas and predefined zones, beginning with already established natural divisions such as cells, dayrooms, and housing unit perimeters, as well as exterior zones. The containment step of the riot plan begins with establishing which doors, gates, or other barriers already exist, determining their methods of operation, understanding their types of operating

mechanisms, ensuring that they are in good working order, and deciding the sequence or manner for using them. The plan should clearly delineate which doors and grilles should be secured in an emergency, and by whom.

By restricting movement in the institution from one zone to another, rioters will be limited in their ability to spread the disturbance directly. Except in those instances where pre-disturbance planning on the part of rioters results in simultaneous takeovers of various parts of the institution, the containment strategy should be useful in stopping a small disturbance from spreading. An intelligent containment plan can sometimes be based on the addition of fast-closing but relatively light steel grilles at key traffic points. These barriers do not have the permanence and mass of outside doors and gates; their prime function is to stop a rush and to gain time to secure the actual containment zones.

Portions of the containment strategy can also rely on low-cost design or traffic pattern changes that are part of the institution's layout. For instance, shop and factory areas where large numbers of inmates are employed (with access to tools that can become weapons in riots) should be divided. This will reduce the number of inmates in each area to a level manageable by the number of officers typically on duty there. A secure metal screen or grille can be used to divide the space, both to maintain visual

> ***By restricting movement in
> the institution from one zone
> to another, rioters will be
> limited in their ability to
> spread the disturbance
> directly.***

supervision and to allow existing heating and ventilating systems to function. Sliding gates can permit the horizontal flow of material and facilitate manufacturing processes.

Other building areas requiring special study are dining halls and gymnasiums, where large groups of inmates may be incited by a few agitators or an otherwise minor incident. Large dining halls seating several hundred men should be avoided whenever possible. In large dining areas, the cafeteria line should ideally flow into several separate spaces isolating the diners into groups of 75 to 100 people. Small dining rooms adjacent to housing units are preferable for maximum security situations.

Exterior Areas

The institution's exterior areas should be carefully analyzed as to arrangement of buildings, circulation routes, and visibility into recreational yards and other areas. Ideally, the pre-identified exterior zones should be rectangular in shape, provide visibility of the complete zone from a guard tower or designated observation point, and provide easy accessibility for staff while being totally secure from assault by the rioters.

Every perimeter post's zone:

■ Should be accessible only under secure custody control
■ Should have safe areas within the zone and evacuation routes for use by staff and inmates escaping the riot
■ Should have closed-circuit television, if possible, to monitor major entrances and exits to areas such as shops, dining rooms, and particularly the exterior zones themselves
■ Should be capable of observing portions of adjacent zones and have voice communication, via intercom, to the control center and other perimeter posts
■ Should have information, on the post, that identifies the location of major electrical and

other utility distribution panels or controls in the zone

Evacuation

All noncorrections personnel (civilians) should be removed from the institution. The advisability of evacuating female staff from isolated posts in medium- and high-security institutions should be considered. The potential for intrusion by outside groups and outside-assisted escapes should not be overlooked in the planning, as such events have occurred in recent years.

Inmates not involved in the disturbance should be kept isolated and at least temporarily restrained, to keep the disturbance to a minimum. These inmates, however, must not be ignored; food, some form of shelter if possible, and necessary medical care should be provided, even if it is while they are kept under armed guard between fences or in a yard area.

Protecting Critical Areas

Control Center

Of special importance is the safety of the control center and its occupants. In a modern facility, the control room is the nerve center of the institution—controlling emergency unlocking of fire exits and operation of the pedestrian sallyports, managing key control, and monitoring the telephone, public address, and institution radio systems. This post also typically maintains radio links with county and state police, monitors perimeter intrusion alarm systems, fence and area lighting, closed-circuit television, and fire alarms, and frequently monitors the alarms on mechanical systems. In short, this is the institution's most critical post.

In the past, the management in some institutions has desired to extend the usefulness of the control center personnel by using the control center officer to directly supervise the lobby, observe the visiting room, or perform similar pure observation and supervision assignments. As a result, architects have designed large glass areas to extend the visual coverage of this post. In general, while some visual monitoring of gates in the immediate area is appropriate, staff in the control room should have few outside supervision responsibilities.

Moreover, recent experience warns that the use of extensive glazing for observation posts, and the dependence on security glazing alone in control centers, are problematic. Where glazing is in place, it should be reinforced with appropriately secure bars. This will prevent inmate penetration during a full-fledged disturbance, where time and the availability of large implements might render a normally secure tempered or laminated glazing vulnerable. The control center is a prime target in an uprising, and it should have reinforced walls, ceiling, and floors, an emergency key drop, bomb-resistant passageways for keys, and the ability to be reinforced by additional staff without unduly jeopardizing the relieving officers.

The control center air conditioning should be 100 percent fresh air. The system should be pressurized to prevent the room from being gassed, and the fan supply unit should be in a secure equipment room. The lighting system in the control center should be on dimmers to allow adjustment of illumination levels for ease in monitoring equipment such as light-emitting diode (LED) signal lights, cathode ray tube screens, closed-circuit television, and other devices.

Access to Keys

To the extent possible, staff should prevent rioting inmates from obtaining security keys and then gaining access to tools and weapons or breaking out of secure areas. It is essential that a set of procedures be implemented to ensure the control of all security keys and locks when an uprising starts. Of vital importance, the control center officer should be able to dispose of security keys through a secure key drop, in the event that area should be likely to fall into inmate hands.

Protective Custody and Segregation Units

Considerable concern must be given to protecting inmates who have requested protection, since in major riots there are inevitably some attempts to kill the "snitches." It is advisable to have a sallyport entrance to any locked unit used to house such cases, so that it can be quickly sealed off. Some alternative emergency exit is also desirable, so that if evacuation is necessary, it can be accomplished into another secure area under staff control. Records for protective custody cases should be maintained in a secure storage area inaccessible to rioters.

In addition, segregation units are commonly a takeover target in a disturbance. This is a special concern because other potential inmate ringleaders are often held there, as well as many other dangerous, violent inmates. The key and sallyport precautions that these units should

might reveal the identity of inmate informants, but loss of inmate records of any type presents serious concerns. Fireproof safes with combination locks, located in a secure area, are highly recommended precautions, even against accidental fire damage.

RESPONSE ISSUES IN LONGER TERM CRISES

For all but the shortest disturbances, a more formal command structure is necessary, and issues like negotiations and use of outside resources come into play.

The control center is a prime

target in an uprising.

already have in place are doubly critical in a riot, since, unlike the protective custody cases, evacuation is ordinarily not an option for these inmates. Response staff should pay particular attention to any inmate activity that indicates a move to take over any locked unit, and be ready to stop it at once.

Other Vital Areas

A second critical concern is the security of areas that may increase the riot's potential severity if they fall into inmate hands. Staff must be immediately aware of the need to secure the hospital drug room, which could provide drugs of various kinds to the rioters; the kitchen and food storage areas, which can provide sustenance; and shop, factory, and warehouse areas where tools and flammable liquids are available. These areas must be secured and controlled as soon as possible to prevent their takeover and exploitation by the insurgents.

Another area that should not be overlooked is the administrative area, where the destruction of records may be an objective. This is a particularly serious concern in those instances where records

Command Center Operations

A primary command center should be set up for all communications and command activity. This may be in a secure area in the institution, but a secondary location outside the perimeter should be identified in the plan, in the event the compound is overrun. This secondary location should not, however, be accessible to the public or the media.

Command center operations should include procedures that ensure all major activities are recorded in a log; audio and telephone recording capability may also be desired. Events logged would include major decisions, significant incoming information, telephone call records, and other key events in the crisis management process. These records would be subject to later court use; they should be legible and chronologically maintained and indicate salient facts such as who originated telephone calls, sources of intelligence, and parties to key decisions. The recorders for these activities should be reliable, highly observant individuals who can be entrusted to not only accurately record events, but to maintain strict confidentiality.

Evidence-gathering equipment is also important, both during and after a riot or hostage situation. Tape recorders should be available to make a record of all telephone calls that take place in the institution, as well as for debriefing staff and inmates. Cameras and video tape equipment allow for valuable documentation of events as they transpire. When available, highly sensitive directional microphones, infrared sensing devices, cameras with telephoto lenses, and other sophisticated equipment can be set up in towers and other key posts to gather intelligence that can be used for operational decisions as well as later prosecution.

Deploying Other Resources

In most disturbances, there is an immediate need for medical equipment and personnel on a standby basis. Medical personnel should be among the first alerted and available, as well as ambulance crews, depending on the seriousness of the incident. Prior agreements with the Red Cross, National Guard, and local medical facilities are a necessary part of pre-emergency planning.

Emergency shelter and sleeping accommodations as well as special food supplies must also be planned for in advance.

Special intelligence-gathering equipment may be necessary in longer sieges, and may be sought from larger law enforcement agencies or the military.

Determining Appropriate Intervention

The most critical decisions to make in a disturbance are the type and timing of any tactical intervention necessary to bring it under control. Key decision makers would ordinarily be the warden, associate or deputy wardens, and the chief of security.

The availability of trained negotiators, staff who are proficient in chemical agents and riot control, a well-disciplined assault force, and a force of skilled marksmen provides flexibility and broad options when faced with a crisis. All of those "teams" should be ready on very short notice, or be available for rapid deployment elsewhere in the correctional system.

Some correctional administrators also feel that it is helpful to have a carefully selected group of people serve as a "think tank" (Cawley 1974) to advise them throughout the disturbance. This group can evaluate in a more detached way the events and facts confronting the administrator. Ideally, they can provide fresh ideas and insights into the crisis and into its solution. This is a particularly valuable strategy when hostages' lives are at stake.

The decisions to be made are likely to include the following: How much risk should be imposed on hostages? Is it proper to negotiate with rioters? When and how much force should be employed?

Rules for Intervention

There are no hard-and-fast rules for such situations; the responsibilities are truly grave. In planning any action, however, the following rules should be observed:

1. Do not make any statement to the group of rioters as to the use of force until you are completely prepared to do so—the attack plans must be completely formulated and response staff must be prepared to carry out any tactical instructions.

2. Give top priority to apprehending any inmate who harms or threatens an employee. Response staff must be sure that these inmates, once taken into custody, are handled in such a manner that prosecution would be possible.

3. Do not attempt a tactical action broader than can be safely handled. A sizeable portion of available response personnel should be held in reserve during the assault action, to allow for unexpected resistance from inmates; to the degree possible, staging areas for these groups should be sufficiently concealed to ensure that the preparations are not observable by either inmates, the media, or the public.[1] Closed vehicles, panel vans, or other windowless types of transport should be considered for moving tactical response staff from a remote staging area to the immediate vicinity of the institution, again so that others cannot determine the extent and nature of any response preparations.

4. Ensure that there are a sufficient number of supervisory staff available, when tactical action begins, to prevent any unprofessional conduct on the part of emotionally charged staff who may see their colleagues and friends injured, or in the worst case, find they have been killed as hostages.

5. Intelligence gathering throughout the crisis should be a high priority, as well as accurate, well-reasoned analysis that can be applied to the decision of whether to assault the institution and how to do so.

6. Squad movements must be worked out in advance, to the degree possible, and coordinated with gas and smoke deployment, which should be used in predetermined quantities and only in specified locations.

7. The manipulation of utilities such as light, water, and heat should be used as strategic and tactical devices.

---

[1]In Atlanta for instance, the institution is in a neighborhood area near a main thoroughfare where it was possible for reporters to see a great deal of the activity near the institution. On one occasion during the Cuban riot, the media observed staff going into the institution during a routine shift change, and erroneously reported that an assault was about to take place. The detainees were monitoring the news, and were dramatically alarmed by this misinformation, which potentially endangered the lives of the staff hostages.

> *Considerable concern must be given to protecting inmates who have requested protection, since in major riots there are inevitably some attempts to kill the "snitches."*

Access Strategies

Once containment is achieved, the ability to quickly regain access to all buildings in the institution is a basic part of restoring control. A plan addressing this factor can begin in many cases with a study of the fire evacuation plan. Using this system in a reverse direction will be effective in reaching many locations.

The emergency key system is a critical component of this part of the plan. Keys should be clearly identified as to which zone they are for, and have some type of coding system to enable staff to identify which key fits which lock. Color coding and notching are two commonly used methods. Moreover, the response tactics must include preparation for cutting through plugged locking devices, removing barricades and otherwise overcoming obstacles to access constructed by the inmates. Environmental controls may have to be disrupted to ensure staff do not deploy gas unnecessarily in noninvolved parts of the institution. Electrical service may have to be shut off to prevent staff from being injured by electrical booby traps. All in all, the access plan must be carefully thought out.

In some cases, an important factor in the riot control plan is the ability to provide fast entry into the institution through the perimeter wall or fence. Many facilities are limited to two entrances—a pedestrian sallyport and a vehicular sallyport. With either of these blocked by the rioters, quick entry becomes a serious problem. Plans must include the possibility of ramming a gate with a truck or heavy equipment, or even possibly landing a tactical force inside the perimeter by helicopter.

If a utilities tunnel system exists in the institution, consideration should be given to connecting the tunnel system with a nearby guard tower that would provide a supervised access point. However, this tunnel also can present a potential avenue of escape for rioters

who may have obtained tools, cutting torches, etc., from shop areas, so it must be secured with that in mind as well.

Internal Communications Issues

Effective communication is critical in controlling riots and disturbances. Administrators should be able to get messages to staff in remote areas, or to isolated groups or even individual inmates. Emergency battery power should be available for low-voltage communications systems. In the event of the total loss of power or destruction of the internal telephone system, the use of bullhorns from strategic points selected in advance may be a necessary element of the communications part of the emergency plan. A public address system should be available to allow communication with groups and to overcome noise and confusion. Hand signals and prearranged smoke grenade signals may also be appropriately used under some circumstances. Advance training or briefing is needed if these latter options are to be effective.

Walkie-talkies should be available to appropriate staff managing the crisis situation. Ideally, a dedicated frequency should be used. For that reason, dual-channel equipment should be considered for the institution. During normal use, the radios carried on the compound by line

staff could be restricted to those units having only one crystal installed. If taken hostage, the second channel could then be safely used by command staff for response activity. Even in nonemergency times, command staff may use the second frequency for sensitive radio traffic, which should not be overheard by line staff. In an emergency, both command personnel and response teams could use dual-channel equipment, enabling them to monitor inmate radio traffic, while permitting secure radio communications between staff members. If possible, staff should consider selecting an alternate radio frequency that is compatible with state police and National Guard equipment.

In some riots, negotiations and other important communications have taken place using radios the rioters seized from staff during the rioting. In this latter instance, all staff-to-staff communications should be confined to frequencies other than the one in the inmates' hands. Unless a totally separate frequency is available, walkie-talkies should generally not be provided rioters if none are in their hands.

Periodic briefings should be held for staff during the crisis, and before any tactical action. Employees should clearly understand what is happening, and to the degree possible, what plans are in place to end the emergency.

The pre-assault briefing is a critical point in the preparation of a crisis response. Topics such as the number, location, and identity of hostages must be covered, as well as barriers in place, numbers of inmates likely to be encountered, types of weapons and protective gear they may have, and other tactical details. In these sessions, supervisory staff should emphasize the need to maintain total professionalism in conducting the tactical action.

Rapid Response in Controlling Disturbances

Disturbances in correctional institutions generally should be resolved as quickly as possible, to minimize the amount of property damage, reduce injury and death, and serve as a deterrent to future uprisings. All things being equal, if the institution has sufficient staff to immediately respond to a hostage situation, the quicker the response, the better.

In hostage situations outside correctional institutions, prolonged negotiations are generally felt to be advisable to permit a phenomenon called the "Stockholm Syndrome" (a strong positive bond between captors and hostages) to occur, which lessens the chance of hostages being killed. Inside correctional institutions, however, relationships already exist between captors and hostages—inmates and staff—which might be highly negative. Therefore, conventional

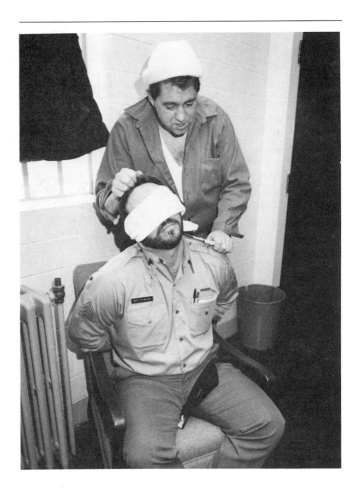

wisdom is that with prolonged time, chances might increase rather than decrease of hostages being physically violated or killed. This argues in favor of a prompt response.

Once again, however, the Oakdale/Atlanta uprisings offer a somewhat different lesson. Over a two-week period, the staff hostages at these two institutions did in fact display some positive affinity to their captors. There are no doubt complex reasons for this, perhaps having to do with the Bureau's humane treatment of the detainees, after their years of adverse conditions in Cuban prisons. But the reason for the distinction between this and other prison hostage situations is not as important as the fact it once again points out—there are no precise answers or predictable outcomes in a prison crisis.

One advantage staff should have in an emergency is that they should be better organized at the outset than the inmates, because of the advance planning and training that should have taken place. The longer a tactical response is delayed, the more opportunity the inmates have to organize, increasing the likelihood of more effective resistance and raising the degree of difficulty in retaking the facility.

Another reason for speed in response is that in most massive riot situations, inmates will

immediately start brewing "hooch," which can take only about 24 hours to ferment. So there is considerable advantage to retaking the institution before the inmates become intoxicated. Furthermore, the longer inmates go without proper supervision, the more likely it is that they will start violently settling old accounts and grievances.

Interestingly, as the uprisings progressed at Attica, Oakdale, and Atlanta, the inmates set up their own internal "police" forces to maintain order. These certainly were not models by any means, but these examples do point out that in lengthier crises, even the inmates begin to develop a sense of the need for order and discipline in their own ranks, if only for protecting hostages who have value as bargaining chips while alive.

Hostage Situations

There has been much discussion, and a great difference of opinion, as to how much risk should be imposed on a hostage or hostages in the process of bringing barricaded rioters to submission. Certainly, a reckless disregard for a hostage's life would not be excused by the public or fellow employees. On the other hand, employment in a correctional institution implies acceptance of the risks that traditionally go with the prison environment, just as is the case with a policeman or soldier. To say that the emergency force should move in with gas and gunfire,

The most critical decisions to make in a disturbance are the type and timing of any tactical intervention.

regardless of risk, would be foolhardy, unless the risk to the public and other innocent people was so great and so imminent as to demand it. Clear tactical orders, hostage location information, briefings on hostage identities using photographs, reminders that hostages may be in inmate uniforms—all these elements must be blended into the response team's preparation for rescuing the hostages. Ongoing intelligence activity is needed throughout the crisis to prepare assault forces with this critical kind of information.

In order to prepare for the possibility of being taken hostage, all correction employees should be trained as to the best and most prudent behavioral responses to such situations. Simulated hostage takings are used to good effect in some correctional systems. These role-play situations are particularly effective with impressionable new employees during pre-service training. Appendix F includes a list of guidelines for this training.

56

Negotiations and Ringleaders

Negotiating during a prison disturbance is a controversial subject. Is it proper to negotiate with rioters? In the past, the answer has, indeed, been a strong "No!" Inmates, in defying the authority of the government, are committing a crime. In addition, any agreements reached under duress would have neither legal nor moral force. This does not imply, however, that some appropriate official should not attempt to talk to the ringleaders in an effort to regain control by peaceful means. This course of action would be particularly germane if hostages were involved, or if the inmates have gained control of some critical point.

In fact, recent incidents have demonstrated success in using a strategy that entails establishing communications, engaging in cautious negotiations, and using prudent judgment in bargaining for the release of hostages, without giving any substantive concessions. However, should discussions fail, the administrator should be prepared to use force in the protection of life or property. Inmates' demands to negotiate only with the governor or some well-known news commentator should be bluntly refused.

An armed rescue is not without risk. In the Attica riot (1971), for example, all of the 11 staff taken hostage died as a result of gunshot wounds inflicted by their would-be rescuers. A Rand study (Jenkins 1977) found that more than 75 percent of all hostages who died were killed during an assault intended to rescue them. The Oakdale/Atlanta incidents provide clear examples of how negotiation brought to a successful conclusion the total takeovers of two major facilities, and the release of over 125 hostages, with none killed and only one seriously injured. Clearly, whether or not to launch an assault is a sobering decision, one where the professional judgment and common sense of a professional correctional administrator have to be given considerable deference.

Negotiation Considerations

The New York State Department of Corrections places considerable emphasis on negotiation, including the selection, training, and utilization of negotiators (Bolz & Hersey 1979 and Wolk & Umina). The following discussion is based, in part, on the experience and work done in New York, but it generally parallels the approach taken by many other agencies.

A special negotiation team should be developed, consisting of people who do not have decision-making authority, and who are not power figures. There are several reasons for this:

1. A power figure is more likely to be injured or taken hostage.
2. The authority to make decisions may put such a person under undue emotional stress, thus increasing the likelihood of making a bad decision.
3. Having someone other than the authority figure as the negotiator buys time and allows consultation in the negotiation process.
4. A nonauthoritative person is less likely to be subject to retaliation if inmates are not pleased with the response.

There should be at least two negotiators, backed up by the decision maker and other resource staff. Mature-appearing males seem to be the most effective in the correctional setting;[2] they must be intelligent and practical and have good verbal skills and proven ability to think clearly under stress. In prisons with numerous Hispanic inmates or when hostage-takers are Hispanic, negotiators should be bilingual in Spanish.[3]

Ideally, negotiations should take place in a secure but private location outside the riot area, to preclude the possibility of theatrics and peer pressure. Some guarantee must be made to ensure the safety of all negotiators, and consideration should be given to conducting negotiations over the telephone or in writing, if necessary.

Generally, negotiations should be conducted without the presence of the media, although the press should be briefed periodically on the progress of negotiations. Caution should be taken so that rigid statements of demands or responses are not released to the media, since these might decrease the likelihood of subsequent concessions, or be misreported, with adverse results.[4] There has, however, been some successful use of the media at the conclusion of negotiations. This has usually been as a final agreement was sealed, or as a concession, in the form of a post-release press statement by the hostage takers. Decisions on the wisdom of such a course must be made as the local situation develops.

Although as previously indicated, there are some ironclad, nonnegotiable rules, these should

---

[2]Since virtually all of the literature on hostage episodes is derived from male institutions, there is no clear recommendation as to negotiators for female hostage takers.

[3]Interestingly, in the Oakdale/Atlanta riots, one institution negotiating team insisted on negotiating in English, at first because the negotiator spoke no Spanish, and later, at least in part, in order to force detainees to put forward a more educated, presumably more reasonable negotiating team. At the other location negotiations were successfully concluded in Spanish.

[4]Also note the prior reference to media misinformation on tactical activity.

longer than a few hours. In this center, the close relatives of the hostages can wait in comfort, and be regularly briefed by institutional staff on the progress of the negotiations or any tactical activity that is going on. Counselors and psychologists can also be available to help family members deal with stress as they wait.

MEDIA RELATIONS

A minor prison disturbance may not create any on-site media interest. However, any major uprising will attract the attention of the news media. Moreover, the presence of the news media is often the first thing inmates demand when there is a more protracted institutional disturbance.

The riot control plan must include a strategy for dealing with the media, so that sensational reporting is discouraged, rumors are dispelled, and misunderstandings are corrected before further tensions are created. An official spokesman must be provided, to ensure timely briefings and an accurate information flow.

It is best to establish a press relations center where dispatches are released and inquiries answered. This will prevent newsmen from roaming about, endangering themselves or others, or gathering fragments of information that could be misreported and jeopardize the negotiations or the hostages' lives. The media center should not be located near the command center or major staff mustering areas, and ideally should be in a training building or other outbuilding where reporters will not interfere with tactical forces or command activities. Media representatives should not become involved in negotiation or riot control activities. Regular briefings by a single agency spokesperson, but not necessarily the warden, will help reduce some of the tensions that occasionally result from a lack of official information.

POST-RIOT ACTIVITIES

As soon as the riot or disturbance has been controlled, the following steps need to be taken:

1. All inmate participants in the riot should be confined to their cells or housing units.

2. An official picture count must be taken of all inmates.

not be stated initially in the discussions between rioters and negotiation team members. That could hinder any subsequent negotiations. Rioters' partial demands should be met only when concessions, such as releasing hostages, providing photos of hostages, or permitting hostage telephone calls, are granted.

If normal telephone communications are not available in a hostage situation, a telephone can be provided to the hostage takers. This will be very helpful in identifying leadership among the hostage takers, providing intelligence information, and monitoring the condition and whereabouts of the hostages. Field telephones or the newer, relatively inexpensive portable telephones provide a fairly effective means of communication, although typical portable telephones based on radio technology are subject to monitoring by the media or other members of the public.

Two other specialized types of equipment are also very desirable. The principal negotiator may, with some caution, consider wearing a small wireless microphone to allow recording any negotiations that take place and to permit prompting from secondary negotiators. Specialized listening devices, or bugs, may be helpful in protracted riot situations to determine rioters' plans, general mood, and the location and condition of hostages. These intelligence-gathering strategies are not without risk; wearing a "hidden" microphone might become counterproductive—even dangerous—if discovered by hostile inmates.

Hostage Families

A hostage family center may also be necessary, in the event a hostage situation lasts

58

Recent incidents have demonstrated success in using a strategy that entails establishing communications, engaging in cautious negotiations, and using prudent judgment in bargaining for the release of hostages.

3. Sufficient staff must be assigned to their supervision to prevent a recurrence of the disturbance.

4. All hostages must be positively identified by a staff member before leaving the secure area of the institution for medical examination and debriefing.

5. All injured people should be immediately evacuated, under proper security procedures.

6. All ringleaders and agitators must be segregated.

7. In most cases, all work and recreation activities should be halted and dining schedules revised, so supervision can be provided for smaller groups during meal periods.

8. Sufficient staff should be provided in quarters and dining rooms, until it is ascertained that the disturbance has been completely suppressed and a more normal atmosphere prevails in the institution.

9. An extensive and thorough investigation should be initiated; this should include interviewing ringleaders and participants in the incident. Normally, rioting inmates should be questioned only by staff who are appointed by

the warden to this task. Individual officers and other staff members should not indiscriminately question inmates who have participated in the riot. If staff have or can obtain closed-circuit television capability to record riot events, it can be used to identify rioters in the act, and then employed afterward in documenting the damage. Procedures should be in place to ensure that any inmates questioned are advised of their constitutional rights, and if possible, sign a form to that effect.

10. Evidence should be secured and properly marked for court use.

11. Employees involved in, or who were witnesses to, the disturbance should immediately be interviewed for statements.

12. Immediate arrangements for repairing the damage of the institution and physical security should be undertaken. All damaged areas should be photographed before they are repaired.

13. The hospital should complete a medical file on all injuries sustained by employees and inmates. Special care should be provided for hostages who might have sustained physical and psychological injury during the disturbance.

14. After returning to normal, staff should be thoroughly debriefed and provided with additional supervisory and perhaps even mental health attention; there should be an awareness of the need to help involved staff to decompress, in order to not create additional problems. In most disturbances, there will be a high percentage of inmates who were not involved, and they should not bear the brunt of residual staff emotions.

15. Both inmates and staff will be tense for some time after a major disturbance. It is obvious that the sooner a relatively normal atmosphere can be restored, the better. Just as soon as it seems safe to do so, the staff should cautiously return to work and other programs can then begin with the objective of restoring the whole institution to normal.

16. A full report of the incident should be compiled, providing an objective critique of the causes of and response to the disturbance; the use of outside parties in such a review should be considered, when the agency head judges it would be beneficial to gain additional objective input into the report.

Conclusion

There are no pat answers, no easy formulas to apply in resolving a prison riot. Each situation is unique and uniquely difficult, and extensive preparation and training are the best safeguards against that moment that every correctional administrator dreads—the sound of the alarm that means a major disturbance is under way.

Considering the havoc, suffering, and costs of riots and disturbances, one cannot fail to notice a certain tragic irony. This is because properly applied management techniques can enable competent administrators to neutralize many of the inherent conditions that can lead to prison disturbances. Unfortunately, despite a well-recognized body of knowledge in this area, there continue to be instances where riots could have been prevented through its timely application, but were not.

Finally, and very importantly, despite the gravity of these crises, administrators must also be concerned about finding a decent and humane response to riotous situations. Our professional ethic demands it be a priority. Indeed, a balanced, professional, appropriately focused response is critical to maintaining public confidence in corrections and in correctional administrators' ability to ensure public safety and institutional security.

Report to the Attorney General

Disturbances at the
Federal Detention Center, Oakdale, LA
and U.S. Penitentiary, Atlanta, GA,
February 1, 1988

RECOMMENDATIONS

The following list of recommendations constitutes a compendium of suggestions and observations believed by the many staff involved in the Atlanta/Oakdale disturbances, as well as the Bureau of Prisons After-Action Team, to be most applicable to large-scale incidents. The Bureau of Prisons has taken the position that they are neither definitive nor universally applicable, and should be regarded as issues and proposals which require additional evaluation as to their utilization in specific institutional settings.

Management

R-1 A formal on-site Command Center organizational structure should be developed as part of a national emergency response plan. One possible structure would consist of the following (list is not necessarily all inclusive):

■ Official in Charge (OIC) Regional Director in the Region where the institution is located; one, possibly two back-ups (Regional Director, Senior Warden) to allow for shift work. This individual would have the advantage of a detachment from the institution and, based on his position, should be able to exert authority over operations.

■ Warden of Institution with one, possibly two back-up Wardens, again to allow for periods of relief.

■ A senior-level official to coordinate security.

■ An experienced staff member responsible for media and public information.

■ A senior-level official to work with hostage families.

■ A senior-level official to coordinate the acquisition of equipment.

■ A senior-level official in charge of the wind-down, including sweep procedures.

■ An official to coordinate disbursement of necessary monies and the issuance of equipment through an outside warehouse.

■ An official to coordinate the assignment of staff.

■ An official in charge of administrative duties (payroll, time and attendance).

■ An official in charge of food service for staff.

■ An official in charge of the negotiation process.

■ An official in charge of inter-agency coordination (contacting other agencies for manpower, equipment, supplies).

■ A sequence monitor (one per shift) to accompany the OIC, taking notes on occurrences.

R-2 Establish plans for a command post/communications center at each institution outside the secure perimeter. If there is a camp adjacent to the institution, recommend the camp inmates be temporarily transferred to another facility. The command post could be established at the camp with support services for staff, such as housing and food being provided at the same location.

R-3 Establish a Regional and Central Office Command Center during an ongoing crisis situation. Representatives from critically involved agencies outside the Bureau of Prisons should be included at the Central Office Command Center.

R-4 A pass system should be used to restrict access to the command/communications center to essential personnel.

R-5 A centralized system should be devised for the deployment of all Bureau of Prisons staff, as well as personnel from other agencies, during any emergency situation.

R-6 Determine circumstances under which Wardens and Regional Directors may provide emergency assistance to agencies outside the Federal Government.

R-7 During any emergency, regular briefings, attended by a senior representative from each agency, should be conducted to correspond with shift changes in order to insure consistency and continuity of decision making and operations.

R-8 Senior level officials or their designees should, on a regular basis, communicate with subordinate staff, providing periodic status reports on the resolution of the emergency situation.

R-9 A mechanism to inform all Bureau of Prisons Chief Executive Officers of developments and pertinent information about disturbances at any Bureau of Prisons facility.

Equipment

R-10 Consider purchasing a portable fluoroscope for use following a disturbance, or during any mass movement of inmates, to ensure that inmates are not concealing contraband.

R-11 Consideration should be given to the purchase of a mobile field kitchen. The kitchen could also be used at those institutions undergoing renovation of food service facilities and during training exercises.

R-12 Establish at least one emergency equipment supply storage center in order to reduce response time in providing critically needed emergency equipment. The following equipment should be included at this central storage facility:

1. Two emergency generators

2. Mobile 25 line telephone system
3. Field kitchen
4. Medical emergency equipment and first aid kits
5. Weapons and ammunition: shotguns, rifles, revolvers, gas, sniper weapons with scopes
6. Security hardware: handcuffs, leg irons, belly chains
7. Riot equipment: batons, helmets, jumpsuits, jackets with "Bureau of Prisons" on front, back and each arm
8. Emergency lighting equipment and search lights
9. Tents, cots, sleeping bags, blankets
10. Portable showers
11. Portable fluoroscope
12. Radios on emergency frequency that cannot be monitored by the public, but have the capability to change frequencies in order to communicate with other agencies
13. Foul weather gear: raincoats, parkas, galoshes, gloves, long underwear
14. Flashlights and batteries
15. Mobile water tank
16. Identification badges/passes/arm bands
17. Portable heaters/fans
18. Bullhorns
19. Administrative supplies
20. Weapon-resistant vests

R-13 Purchase and equip at least one mobile command post with necessary communication gear and station it at a centralized location for immediate deployment.

R-14 Explore possibility of locating the mobile command/communication center and tractor trailers containing disturbance control equipment and other emergency supplies on an Air Force Base where the Bureau operates a correctional facility, such as Eglin AFB, or Vandenburg AFB, so that the equipment can be quickly transported by military aircraft such as a C5-A.

R-15 Memoranda of understanding should be developed between the Bureau of Prisons and other agencies such as the FBI, INS, U.S. Marshal's Service and the Department of Defense. These agreements should specify the conditions under which the agency would assist the Bureau of Prisons during emergency situations such as a major disturbance, and describe the kind of assistance that a particular agency might extend to the Bureau.

R-16 Ensure there is a system for the accountability of weapons and other supplies used during a disturbance, to provide for their return to the loaning agency or institution.

R-17 Develop specifications for use of explosives to gain entry through various types of security doors and locks used throughout the Bureau of Prisons. Maintain this information in the armory or outside Command Center at each institution, and a compilation of all such specifications in the Regional Office.

R-18 All institutions should make an annual assessment to ensure adequacy of emergency response equipment such as weapons, tear gas, gas masks, batons, flashlights and field jackets.

R-19 Each institution should place a portable base radio in the armory or outside Command Center.

R-20 Determine if there is existing technology that would enable staff to "jam" regular institution radios so that inmates cannot use them.

R-21 Consult with the Federal Emergency Management Agency (FEMA) to determine what assistance and equipment they might provide during a disturbance or other emergency.

R-22 Office of Technology should assess the need for communication and surveillance equipment in Bureau of Prisons' institutions. A determination should be made on what equipment and resources are available from other Federal agencies for use by the Bureau of Prisons.

R-23 An adequate number of jackets should be maintained at each institution with "Bureau of Prisons" marked in large letters on the front, back and each sleeve. All staff (including non-Bureau of Prisons staff) involved in an emergency situation should be easily identifiable via jacket and badge or pass.

R-24 Wardens and Bureau of Prisons Executive Staff members should have portable mobile phones. These phones would allow immediate contact and insure continuity of contact while one is enroute to an institutional emergency. Also, it would facilitate communication in the event regular telephone service was interrupted during an emergency.

R-25 Explore the possibility of renting a satellite audio remote service to provide communication from the disturbance site to the Central Office.

Security

R-26 Include procedures in emergency plans for establishing and maintaining the secure perimeter of the institution that can be immediately put into action in any emergency situation.

R-27 Emergency plans should specify perimeter posts that are to be manned during an emergency.

R-28 Institutional emergency plans need to include contact points with utility companies, as well as with suppliers of communication equipment and other equipment that might need to be rented or purchased during an emergency situation of some magnitude.

R-29 Emergency plans should be developed at the Regional and Central Office levels, outlining the command structure that will be used in major emergencies, as well as assigning responsibilities for deploying manpower and other resources.

R-30 Each institution should identify in emergency plans, boundaries for public access, a media center, and areas for staging supplies, personnel, equipment, hostage families (off the institution grounds) and debriefing.

R-31 A copy of the institution disturbance control plan should be maintained in the institution armory or the outside emergency Command Center.

R-32 Each institution's disturbance control plan should be reviewed annually, and that review should include consultation with representatives of other agencies involved in the plan. Review of such plans should be part of the audit process.

R-33 Architectural drawings showing all utilities, tunnels, and access areas should be maintained in an area outside the perimeter and at the Regional and Central Offices. Video tapes should be made of all areas of the institution to supplement these architectural designs. These video tapes and drawings must be kept current to reflect modifications in the structures. Aerial photographs should also be maintained by the institution with copies in the Regional and Central Office.

R-34 Ensure the capacity to control all utilities (electricity, water, natural gas) to various areas of the institution. Shut-off capacity should be located outside the perimeter of the institution.

R-35 Specific oversight procedures aimed at minimizing the potential for actual or alleged abuse of inmates should be developed for processing inmates during and after any disturbance.

R-36 Greater consideration should be given to the compatibility of a particular UNICOR product line with the security level and mission of an institution. The detainees in Atlanta used knives in their work. Also, the type and quantity of materials stored precluded thorough searches of the factory for weapons and other contraband.

R-37 Evaluate the security of Control Centers and front entrances in all institutions, particularly those designed similar to the Oakdale facility, to determine the extent to which these areas might be vulnerable to assaults both from outside and inside the institution.

R-38 All Bureau institutions should have

special housing capabilities. For example, Oakdale had no segregation unit, which restricted the options available to staff in handling disciplinary infractions.

R-39 In order to facilitate the issuance of firearms during an emergency, a list of staff who are qualified to use weapons should be maintained outside the secure perimeter of the institution.

R-40 Prior to any change in an institution's mission, the physical plant of the institution should be modified, where necessary, to meet any increased need for security.

R-41 An evaluation of the location and security for institution tool rooms should be made and reviewed periodically.

R-42 When issuing weapons at the time of a disturbance, specific instructions should be offered on the circumstances under which weapons will be used.

R-43 Review the legal issues related to the use of weapons, by agencies outside the Federal Government, during emergency situations involving Federal property and Federal prisoners.

R-44 During a post disturbance "sweep," ensure that an electrician, plumber, physician's assistant and other appropriate staff be on site to provide immediate assistance.

R-45 No uniform clothing should be stored inside the secure perimeter of an institution and guidelines should be developed for staff personal items permitted inside the institution.

R-46 Extra emergency keys should be maintained in the armory or outside command post.

R-47 Develop instructions for the immediate disposal of medications in the event the security of the pharmacy is seriously threatened during a disturbance.

Hostage Negotiations

R-48 During a hostage situation, negotiators' superiors should arrange for periodic briefings of the hostage families and support staff on the status of the negotiations.

R-49 Whenever possible, negotiators should be advised in advance by command decision-makers of the intended movement and deployment of tactical assault teams.

R-50 Every effort should be made during a hostage situation to prevent inmates from communicating with the outside world. Access to the news media may impede the negotiation process and hamper a speedy resolution.

R-51 When appropriate during a hostage situation, inmates should be told of planned actions that they may perceive as aggressive or threatening. For example, a tense situation arose at Oakdale when staff wanted to enter the rear

sallyport to retrieve an item. The detainees apparently perceived this as a potential assault and some hostages were consequently threatened.

R-52 While it may not be desirable for the Bureau of Prisons to independently handle hostage negotiations, there should be a few designated Bureau employees who are highly trained with the expertise to lead or serve as a member of a negotiating team.

R-53 As a general rule, the role of third parties in a hostage situation should be clearly limited to consultation in the negotiation process.

R-54 No staff members, other than those involved in negotiations, should be permitted to talk to inmates involved in a disturbance.

Policy Revisions

R-55 In the event of an institution takeover or major disturbance, the next higher level of authority should assume command of the situation.

R-56 Establish minimum inventory requirements for emergency equipment for each security level. For example, the amount of tear gas maintained at the higher security level institutions, in particular, may need to be increased.

R-57 Establish Special Operations Response Teams (SORT) at all Level 4, 5 and 6 institutions. National policy should outline minimum standards for training and equipment, and stipulate the requirement that emergency equipment accompany TDY staff.

R-58 Policy guidelines should be developed for institutional emergency plans in order to ensure a degree of standardization and sufficient detail. Plans should be approved initially by the Central and Regional Offices and reviewed as part of the audit process. Other agencies, the FBI in particular, should be consulted on the development of such plans. Care must be taken so that individual plans accurately reflect the availability of resources at a particular institution.

R-59 Legal options for controlling access to private property adjacent to institutional property should be explored.

Media

R-60 Select one or more National Public Information Officers capable of dealing with the national media. These individuals should have field experience in the Bureau of Prisons and should be expertly trained in dealing with the media. They should also have a basic understanding of the hostage negotiation process. These PIO's should be used throughout the Bureau during emergency situations, and be available to clarify information propagated by inmates, the media and the public.

R-61 Establish a Public Education Office to allow for a more centralized, proactive response to the media. This should enhance the public's understanding of the Bureau and may assist in recruiting efforts.

R-62 During an emergency, press releases should address issues of both national and local interest.

R-63 Where appropriate, provide press releases in both English and foreign languages.

R-64 Attempt to make press releases or status reports at specific times using a designated agency official at a centralized location.

R-65 During a major disturbance, consideration should be given to establishing an "800" number to be used to provide information and dispel rumors.

Hostages and Hostage Families

R-66 Duplicate the program which was established at both Oakdale and Atlanta for dealing with hostages and their families to include organizational records-keeping, staff responsibilities, communication of information to families, and opportunities for families to participate in the operation of the program.

R-67 Ensure the development of a specific procedure to provide timely notification to an employee's family by a mid-level or senior-level staff member, in the event of a hostage situation. This procedure should also provide for periodic updates to the hostage family members until the situation is resolved.

R-68 Photos or video tapes made of hostages should be shown to hostage family members. Psychological staff should edit these video tapes for elimination of counter therapeutic content prior to family viewing.

R-69 Ensure that standard FBI hostage release protocol is not followed as regards pat searches and handcuffing, when the hostage is an identified Bureau of Prisons staff member.

R-70 The Bureau of Prisons should plan for the reintroduction of former hostages to the work place, facilitation of appropriate job changes, short and long range educational and psychological support for former hostages and their families.

R-71 Materials should be developed which speak to the stress experienced by children, with emphasis on parents managing children's stress-generated behavior.

R-72 Consideration should be given to broadening incident stress debriefing for staff other than hostages who are intimately involved in a disturbance.

R-73 A hostage who is released, while other hostages are still being held, should not be permitted to return to work until the disturbance is resolved.

Training

R-74 Evaluate the adequacy of disturbance control training offered at the Staff Training Academy and the institutions.

R-75 Training programs should include developing increased sensitivity to indicators of institution unrest, such as subtle changes in inmate behavior.

R-76 Consideration should be given to developing training exercises on dealing with disturbances and other emergencies, and incorporating them into annual refresher training.

R-77 Provide training on what to expect in hostage situations and concomitant coping techniques. This training could be conducted by psychologists, chaplains, negotiators, and, perhaps, include videotaped experiences described by hostages. Refresher training on this topic should also be provided.

R-78 Develop staff training programs aimed at sensitizing staff to cultural differences among various inmate groups and how these differences affect interactions among various groups.

R-79 All Bureau of Prisons' Executive Staff members and Wardens should be trained in the basic philosophies underlying the hostage negotiation process, and the Bureau's disturbance policies.

R-80 Training programs in the use of force, both at the Staff Training Academy and the institution, need to clarify the conditions under which force will be used on detainees and pre-trial defendants, as opposed to sentenced inmates.

Records/Administration

R-81 Current photographs and telephone numbers of employees (including contract and Public Health Service employees) should be maintained in a secure location outside the secure perimeter. Employees should be strongly encouraged to provide telephone contacts in addition to immediate family members.

R-82 All confidential investigative records and files pertaining to both staff and inmates should be maintained outside the secure perimeter of the institution.

R-83 When there is a disturbance or other emergency situation, chronological logs briefly depicting events should be established immediately. A specific staff member should be assigned this responsibility as part of the command post structure.

R-84 Contemporary logs should be

maintained of all command-related decisions and discussions (including phone calls), both internal and with the Regional and Central Office. Key documents should be dated, marked as to time, and maintained for ready reference. A reading file should be established to enable staff coming on duty to familiarize themselves readily with events. If possible, all radio transmissions during any emergency situation should be logged.

R-85 Assemble a portable emergency kit at each institution which would include logbooks, blank rosters, purchase orders, etc. This kit should be stored outside the perimeter of the institution.

R-86 Wherever possible, critical information such as inmate commissary accounts and sentence computation records should be placed in a computer system so that data are retrievable from outside the perimeter of the institution.

R-87 An appropriate number of photographers and video camera operators should be available at all times during an emergency situation to document activities. All photos and tapes should be identified by date and location.

Future Construction

R-88 Design and situate Control Centers so as to minimize vulnerability to assaults from both outside and inside the institution. Control Centers should be located outside the secure perimeter.

R-89 Locate food storage warehouse outside secure perimeter.

R-90 Locate central tool room in sallyport area of rear gate entrance.

R-91 Powerhouse, including emergency generator, should be located outside the secure perimeter.

R-92 Establish the capacity to control from the outside all utilities, i.e., electricity, water and natural gas, in various areas of the institution inside the secure perimeter.

R-93 Consider the advisability of constructing towers in Level 4 & 5 institutions.

R-94 Have separate water loops outside the perimeter with master valves to ensure a water supply for fire control.

R-95 All future satellite camps should be constructed to be as self-sufficient as economically feasible. For example, no utilities should be fed through the main institution.

R-96 Have the Office of Technology determine the feasibility of adding security to high-mast lights so inmates cannot tamper with them.

R-97 Construction methods for walls in high security areas should be evaluated to reduce the possibility of circumventing security doors and grilles.

R-98 Security cell doors should have a sliding rail design rather than the swinging hinged type.

R-99 New institutions should be constructed so that the Administration Building is built as part of the main institution, but physically outside the secure perimeter. Consideration should be given to an FCI, Butner, N.C., type design rather than a detached Administration Building within the secure perimeter.

Staff Services

R-100 The Department of Labor should be contacted as soon as possible after a disturbance begins and hostages are taken to request assistance in expediting the processing of workmen's compensation claims.

R-101 The Food Service Supervisor should be provided regular briefings and be notified by the official in charge of staffing of the number of people on duty to ensure that an adequate food supply is available.

R-102 Institution Food Service Administrators should determine what resources are available in the local community for providing staff meals during a disturbance or other disaster.

R-103 During an emergency situation, arrangements should be made for off-duty staff to be housed away from the institution so that they are better able to rest.

R-104 There should be a consistent policy on compensation issues, such as overtime, whether staff are in Central Office, Regional Office or at the site of a disturbance.

Fire Safety

R-105 Determine, to the extent possible, how well the sprinkler systems operated during the disturbances at Atlanta and Oakdale.

R-106 Determine the capacity to shut off the water supply inside the institution while maintaining the supply for use at the institution's perimeter.

R-107 Insure that each institution has a mutual aid agreement with the local fire department. Where such a plan exists, review the adequacy of the agreement for various levels of emergency.

APPENDIX B

ACA Standards Related to Riots and Disturbances in Correctional Institutions*

2-4014 Written policy and procedure provide for meetings to be held at least monthly between the warden/superintendent and all department heads, and meetings to be held at least monthly between department heads and their key staff members. (Essential)

DISCUSSION: Channels of communication should be used for delegating authority, assigning responsibility, supervising work, and coordinating efforts. Designated channels of communication, both vertical and lateral, should govern the activities and working relationships of institution personnel.

2-4015 Written policy and procedure provide for a system of two-way communication between all levels of staff and inmates. (Essential)

DISCUSSION: Good communication between staff and inmates is necessary for the efficient operation of the institution and may reduce reliance on grievance mechanisms.

2-4020 Written policy and procedure provide for the institution to report in writing its activities at least quarterly to the parent agency. Reports include major developments in each department or administrative unit, major incidents, population data, staff and inmate morale, and major problems and plans for solving them. (Essential)

DISCUSSION: Routine reporting by individual institutions in a multi-institution system

permits top management personnel to stay informed about current programs, activities, and problems throughout the system. The exchange of reports among institutions permits an opportunity for joint problem-solving. Major incidents are those which require written reports similar to those required for major rule violations.

2-4022 The institution provides for all inmates the following constructive programs, including, at a minimum: reception and orientation; evaluation and classification; academic education equivalent to high school; vocation training; employment; religious services; social services and counseling; psychological and psychiatric services; library services; medical and dental health care; athletic, recreational and leisure time activities; inmate involvement with community groups; mail and visiting; access to media, legal materials, attorneys and courts; volunteer services; and prerelease orientation and planning. (Essential)

DISCUSSION: The institution should request sufficient funding and staff to provide for inmates' activities that afford them opportunity for improvement.

2-4024 Written policy and procedure provide for a public information program that encourages

*American Correctional Association. 1981. *Standards for Adult Correctional Institutions, Second Edition.* College Park, Md.: American Correctional Association.

67

contacts with the public and communications media. (Essential)

DISCUSSION: A planned and continuing public information and education program can help the community and news media understand the goals, purposes and role of the institution and may lead to greater community involvement and support.

2-4025 Written policy and procedure provide for granting representatives of the media access to the institution, consistent with the preservation of inmates' privacy and the maintenance of order and security. (Essential)

DISCUSSION: None. (Related Standard 2-4339)

2-4056 There is an affirmative action program that has been approved by the appropriate government agency. (Essential)

DISCUSSION: An affirmative action program should contain necessary guidelines to accomplish the public policy goal of equal employment opportunity. For example, all persons should be able to compete equally for entry into, and promotion within the institution. The program should also be designed to seek out qualified minority groups and women in order to encourage their participation in the staff development program of the institution. The program should include corrective actions, when needed, in policies regarding rate of pay, demotion, transfer, layoff, termination, and upgrading.

2-4059 Written policy and procedure make provision for the employment of qualified ex-offenders. (Important)

DISCUSSION: Ex-offenders can be a valuable manpower resource and should not be discriminated against when they seek employment with an institution. A program of selection, orientation, in-service training, constructive supervision, and opportunity for advancement can provide the institution a valuable manpower resource. (Related Standard 2-4061)

2-4088 Written policy and procedure provide that all new full-time employees receive 40 hours of orientation/training prior to being independently assigned to a particular job. This orientation/training is to include, at a minimum, orientation to the purpose, goals, policies and procedures of the institution and parent agency; working conditions and regulations;

responsibilities and rights of employees; and an overview of the corrections field. Depending upon the employee(s) and the requirements of the particular job, the orientation/training may include some preparatory instruction related to the particular job. There are provisions for acknowledging and giving credit for prior training received. (Essential)

DISCUSSION: None. (Related Standard 2-4174)

2-4090 Written policy and procedure provide that all support employees who have regular or daily inmate contact receive an additional 40 hours of training during their first year of employment and an additional 40 hours of training each subsequent year of employment. (Essential)

DISCUSSION: Food service, industrial supervisors, and other support personnel who, as a part of their job requirements, have day to day contact with inmates should receive specialized training to supplement their particular area of expertise. These individuals should be familiar with policies and procedures of the institution, plus the basic rules of inmate supervision and security. Ongoing training during subsequent years of employment enables employees to sharpen skills and keep abreast of changes in operational procedures. (See related Standards 2-4174 and 2-4210)

2-4091 Written policy and procedure provide that all professional specialists employees who have inmate contact receive an additional 40 hours of training during their first year of employment, and an additional 40 hours of training each subsequent year of employment. (Essential)

DISCUSSION: Casemanagers, chaplains, teachers, medical personnel, etc., all have received considerable training and education in their field prior to qualifying for a particular position. However, they should receive orientation and training relative to the policies, procedures and regulations of the institution, as well as specific training in their area as it relates to an institutional environment. Ongoing training during subsequent years of employment enables employees to sharpen skills and keep abreast of new developments in their respective fields, as well as changes in operational procedures. (Related Standards 2-4174 and 2-4210)

2-4092 Written policy and procedure provide that all new correctional officers receive an additional 120 hours of training during their first year of employment and an additional 40 hours of training each subsequent year of employment. At a minimum this training covers the following areas:

Security procedures
Supervision of inmates
Use of force regulations and tactics
Report writing
Inmate rules and regulations
Rights and responsibilities of inmates
Fire and emergency procedures
Firearms training
Key control
Interpersonal relations
Social/cultural life styles of the inmate population
Communication skills
First aid. (Essential)

DISCUSSION: Since the duties of correctional officers frequently involve most institutional operations, their training should be comprehensive. Ongoing training during subsequent years of employment enables employees to sharpen skills and keep abreast of changes in operational procedure. (Related Standards 2-4096, 2-4174, 2-4196, 2-4285, 2-4346, and 2-4347)

2-4093 Written policy and procedure provide that all administrative and managerial staff receive an additional 40 hours of training during their first year of employment, and an additional 40 hours of training each subsequent year of employment. This training covers, at a minimum: general management and related subjects; labor law; employee-management relations; the interaction of elements of the criminal justice system; and relationships with other service agencies. (Essential)

DISCUSSION: Administrative and managerial staff should receive training that enables them to respond effectively to problems, and to deal effectively with the parent agency, the employees, and the community.

2-4094 When there is an emergency unit, written policy and procedure provide that all assigned officers have one year of experience as a correctional officer, which includes 160 hours of training; that they receive 40 hours of relevant emergency unit training prior to assignment, which may be part of the first year training (160 hours), and that at least 16 hours of the 40 hours of annual training be specifically related to emergency unit assignment. (Essential)

DISCUSSION: As knowledge of handling emergency situations increases, many agencies are creating emergency units, sometimes called "squads," "confrontation units," and the like. Members of these units should receive training that will enable them to implement new knowledge and techniques, to include procedures to be followed in hostage situations. (See related Standard 2-4092 and 2-4211)

2-4096 Prior to assignment to a post involving possible use of a firearm, all personnel authorized to use firearms receive appropriate firearm training; this training covers the use, safety, care, and constraints involved in the use of firearms. All authorized personnel are required to demonstrate competency on at least an annual basis. (Mandatory)

DISCUSSION: Staff authorized to use firearms require thorough training in their use, safety, and care. A specific curriculum should be established that includes individual and group instruction by competent authorities. Instructions should include training regarding the limited conditions under which the use of firearms would be condoned; this training should be comparable to the police constraints or regulations of that particular jurisdiction. (Related Standard 2-4092 and 2-4186)

2-4097 All personnel authorized to use chemical agents are thoroughly trained in their use and in the treatment of individuals exposed to the chemical agent. (Mandatory)

DISCUSSION: Chemical agents, if not properly used and handled, could result in serious injury. A special curriculum should be established that includes both individual and group instruction by competent authorities. Personnel from the military, the Federal Bureau of Investigation, and the state and local police could provide the instruction.

2-4098 All security and custodial personnel are trained in approved methods of self-defense and the use of force as a last resort to control inmates. (Essential)

DISCUSSION: It is sometimes necessary to use physical force to control and/or move inmates. All security and custodial personnel should be trained in the techniques by which this can be done with minimal harm and discomfort to the inmates and staff.

2-4170 The institution has equipment necessary to maintain essential lights, power and communications in an emergency. (Essential)

DISCUSSION: The institution should have emergency power units, either battery or motor driven, to provide essential lighting and to maintain the life-sustaining functions within the institution and to continue communications with outside interests. (Related Standard 2-4213)

2-4171 Power generators are tested at least every two weeks and other emergency equipment and systems are tested at least every quarter for effectiveness and are repaired or replaced if necessary. (Essential)

DISCUSSION: Frequent checks of emergency equipment, such as standby lighting, batteries, power generators, fire fighting apparatus, communications systems and alarms, ensure their reliability in time of need. (Related Standards 2-4151 and 2-4164)

2-4172 The institution has a written evacuation plan prepared in the event of fire or major emergency which is certified by an independent, outside inspector trained in the application of national fire safety codes. The plan is reviewed annually, updated if necessary, and reissued to the local fire jurisdiction. The plan includes the following:

Location of building/room floor plans
Use of exit signs and directional arrows for traffic flow
Location of publicly posted plan
At least quarterly drills in all institution locations
Staff drills when evacuation of extremely dangerous inmates may not be included. (Mandatory)

DISCUSSION: The evacuation plan should also specify routes of evacuation, subsequent disposition and housing of inmates, and provision for medical care or hospital transportation for injured inmates and/or staff. Fire drills should include evacuation of all inmates except when there is clear and convincing evidence that institutional security is jeopardized. Upon such showing, actual evacuation during drills is not required, although staff supervising such inmates should be required to perform their roles/activity in quarterly drills. (Related Standard 2-4134)

2-4174 All institution personnel are trained in the implementation of written emergency plans. (Mandatory)

DISCUSSION: Review of all emergency plans should be an essential element of personnel training and retraining programs. New employees should be familiar with all emergency plans prior to permanent work assignment.

2-4186 Written policy and procedure govern the use of firearms, to include the following:

Weapons are subjected to stringent safety regulations and inspections.
Except in emergency situations, employees carrying firearms are assigned only to watch towers, gun walks, mobile patrols, or other positions that are inaccessible to inmates.
Employees supervising inmates outside the institution perimeter follow procedures which specify methods for ensuring the security of weapons.
Employees are instructed to use deadly force only after other actions have been tried and found ineffective, unless the employee believes that a person's life is immediately threatened.
Employees on duty use only firearms issued by the institution and use them only when directed by or authorized by the warden/superintendent or officer in charge. (Mandatory)

DISCUSSION: In order to reduce the risk of firearms falling into the hands of inmates, institution personnel who spend most of their time in direct personal contact with inmates must not carry firearms. Use of firearms in transporting inmates or in outside work assignments requires officers who are trained in the handling and use of firearms. (Related Standard 2-4096)

2-4188 Written policy and procedure govern the availability, control, and use of firearms, ammunition, chemical agents and related security devices, and specify the level of authority required for access to and use of security devices. Chemical agents are used only at the direction of the warden/superintendent or designee. (Essential)

DISCUSSION: Designated staff should determine, based on an analysis of the physical plant and number and profile of the inmate population, what firearms, chemical agents, and other security devices (such as shields, batons, helmets, gloves, body protectors, etc.) the institution needs. Written policies and procedures should specify the level of authority required for access to and use of security devices. Chemical agents should be used only at the direction of the warden/superintendent or delegated subordinate.

2-4189 Firearms, chemical agents and related security equipment are stored in a secure but readily accessible depository outside inmate housing and activity areas, and are inventoried at least monthly to determine their condition and expiration dates. (Essential)

DISCUSSION: The institution should maintain an arsenal for the secure storage and maintenance of all its firearms, ammunition, chemical agents, and other security devices. The arsenal should be located outside the inmate housing and activities area. Written policy should specify who has access to the arsenal.

2-4190 Written policy and procedure provide that the institution maintains a written record of routine and emergency distributions of security equipment. (Essential)

DISCUSSION: A written record detailing who receives security equipment and what equipment they receive is necessary to establish responsibility and accountability for its use.

2-4191 Written policy and procedure require that personnel discharging firearms, using chemical agents or any other weapon, or using force to control inmates submit written reports to the warden/superintendent or designee no later than the conclusion of the tour of duty. (Essential)

DISCUSSION: All instances involving the discharge of firearms and use of chemical agents should be documented to establish the identity of personnel and inmates involved and to describe the nature of the incident.

2-4203 Written policy and procedure require the chief security officer to inspect at least weekly, and report in writing, all security devices needing repair or maintenance. (Essential)

DISCUSSION: There should be a scheduled maintenance procedure to ensure that all bars, locks, windows, doors, and other security devices are fully operational. Emergency keys should be checked at least quarterly to make sure that they are in working order. Results of all inspections should be submitted in writing to the chief executive officer and/or the officer in charge of security. (Related Standard 2-4151)

2-4206 Written policy and procedure restrict the use of physical force to instances of justifiable self-protection, defense of others, protection of property, and prevention of escapes, as a last resort and in accordance with appropriate statutory authority. In no event is physical force justifiable as punishment. A written report is prepared following all uses of force and is submitted to the administrative staff for review. (Mandatory)

DISCUSSION: Correctional personnel should be prepared to justify their use of physical force. In no case should force be considered justifiable as punishment or discipline.

2-4208 Written policy and procedure provide that all persons injured in an incident receive an immediate medical examination and treatment. (Mandatory)

DISCUSSION: In all instances involving the use of a weapon or chemical agent, immediate medial examination and treatment should be required for the protection of all staff and inmates involved.

2-4210 There are written plans that specify procedures to be followed in situations which threaten institutional security, including, but not limited to, riots, hunger strikes, disturbances, and taking of hostages. These plans are made available to all applicable personnel and reviewed and updated at least annually. (Mandatory)

DISCUSSION: The plans should designate the personnel who are to implement such procedures, when and which authorities and media should be notified, how the problem should be contained, and what should be done after the incident is quelled. The plans presuppose regular inspection and maintenance of specialized equipment necessary to implement the procedures. All personnel should become familiar with the plans. Hospital and medical personnel should be involved in the formulation of the written plans, since they are responsible for the safety of their patients. (Related Standards 2-4090, 2-4091, and 2-4092)

2-4211 Where there is a special unit of employees to assist in the event of disturbances, those employees are selected and evaluated according to written criteria and receive special training in methods of negotiation and confrontation. (Important)

DISCUSSION: A small unit of selected employees should receive special training in methods of confrontation and negotiation. The purpose of this unit should be to restore order, with minimum damage, as quickly as possible. Therefore, unit members should be selected carefully and trained in the performance of these special duties. Their performance evaluation should be based upon the specific aspects of the special duty. The unit should be activated only by the warden/superintendent or designee. (Related Standard 2-4094)

2-4343 There is a written inmate grievance procedure which is made available to all inmates and which includes at least one level of appeal. (Essential)

DISCUSSION: A grievance procedure is an administrative means for the expression and resolution of inmate problems. The institution's grievance mechanism should include the following: provision for written responses to all grievances, including the reasons for the decision; provision for response within a prescribed, reasonable time limit, with special provisions for responding to emergencies; provision for supervisory review of grievances; provision for participation by staff and inmates in the design and operation of the grievance procedure; provision for access by all inmates, with guarantees against reprisals; applicability over a broad range of issues; and, means for resolving questions of jurisdiction.

2-4401 The system for classifying inmates specifies the level of custodial control required and requires a regular review of each classification. (Essential)

DISCUSSION: A correctional system should provide for at least three degrees of custodial control for inmates. All inmates should be assigned the least restrictive custodial level necessary.

APPENDIX C

Qualifications for Special Response Teams

The following is a list of suggested considerations for forming, qualifying, and training an institutional special response team.

TEAM COMPOSITION

Each team will be composed of the following members:

- 1 team commander, who is ordinarily the chief of the institution's security force
- 2 team leaders, who are usually supervisory staff in the security force
- 12 team members, who may be drawn from any department in the institution
- Alternates, as determined locally

QUALIFICATIONS

- Completion of any probationary period required by the agency.
- Successful completion of a full physical examination, which should include rigorous exercise and an assessment of physical stress capacity.
- Ability to perform specified physical tasks, such as completion of a two-mile run in 18 minutes, completion of 50 situps nonstop, completion of 35 push-ups nonstop, and completion of an obstacle course within an established time, if one is available.
- Technical qualifications as follows: Weapons proficiency; rappelling; riot control techniques; tactical response proficiency; and policy knowledge in areas of use of force, application of restraints, arresting authority, use of chemical agents, and all institution emergency plans.
- Complete successfully a personal interview

with the warden or designee, team commander, team leaders, and institution psychologist. The purpose of these teams is to avoid confrontation and reduce the seriousness of a crisis, not to feed it through an exaggerated or imprudent response. Consequently, these staff should have a history of personal stability, reliability, and use of good judgment in the prison environment, and particularly in emergency situations.

SPECIAL SKILL AREAS

Each team member should be required to be a specialist in one or more of the following areas: Emergency medical treatment (ordinarily limited to medical staff on the team); blueprint reading for tactical purposes; advanced ability in security hardware, locking systems and cutting equipment; sharpshooting; rappelling; tactical planning and plan execution; and assault weapons use.

TRAINING

All team members must be provided monthly training, as a team. This should consist of eight hours each month, plus an additional eight hours annually, of mock exercises and 40 hours annually in intense tactical training. The medical specialist and alternate team members should receive 16 hours training per quarter with the team and participate in the annual mock training.

All training will be certified monthly by the warden, associate warden, commander, and leaders. All documentation on training and the complete roster of team members will be maintained by the commander.

Indicators of Prison Tension That Often Precede Riots and Disturbances

Disturbances in correctional institutions can be prevented if staff are able to interpret and act on changes in the institutional atmosphere and behavior patterns. Among the signs indicating growing tensions and potential disturbances are the following:

- Increased separation by racial or ethnic groups
- Increased purchases of foodstuffs at inmate canteens
- Increased requests for transfers
- Decrease in the number of workers
- Many inmates spending more time in their cells
- Inmate groupings with point men facing away from the group
- Increase in disciplinary cases
- Increase in inmate/employee confrontations
- Increase in inmates trying to intimidate officers who are in the process of writing up an inmate
- Increase in veiled threats against officers
- Increase in voluntary lockups
- Increase in inmate sick calls
- Increase in inmate violence

- Increase in number of weapons found in shakedowns
- Harsh stares from inmates
- Drop in attendance at movies or other popular functions
- Unusual and/or subdued actions by inmate groups
- Reluctance on the part of inmates to communicate with staff
- Inmates avoiding eye contact with staff
- Inmates making excessive and/or specific demands
- Appearance of inflammatory and anti-authority materials
- Warnings to "friendly" officers to take sick leave or vacation
- Increased safety demands from employees
- Significant increase in employee resignations
- Letters and/or telephone calls from concerned inmate families demanding protection for inmates
- Unusual number of telephone inquiries about prison conditions
- Outside agitation

APPENDIX E

Sample Riot Response Plan

DISTURBANCE CONTROL PROCEDURE
SECURITY AND CONTROL
SECURITY POLICY 310-100

I. AUTHORITY: This policy is issued in compliance with the orders of the director of the Department of Corrections. It is also issued in accord with [statutory authority], which delegates to the warden authority to manage and direct all inmates, personnel, volunteers, programs, and activities connected with the institution.

II. PURPOSE: This order provides general guidelines for the clarification of roles, responsibilities and procedures in the event of a disturbance at the [Name] Correctional Institution.

III. APPLICABILITY: This policy is applicable to all employees of the [Name] Correctional Institution and especially to those employees involved in activities relating to the effective containment and resolution of disturbances at the [Name] Correctional Institution.

IV. DEFINITIONS: None

V. POLICY: It is the policy of the [Name] Correctional Institution to use a proactive approach to prevent disturbances through proper use of communication skills, security procedures, and preparedness. It is further the policy of this institution to respond quickly with only the force necessary to control any disturbance that might occur.

100-01: RESPONSIBILITIES:

100-01.01: It is the responsibility of [Name] Correctional Institution warden to develop a disturbance control plan and to conduct an annual review of the plan to ensure its accuracy. All agencies providing assistance as part of the institution plan will be invited to attend the annual review.

100-01.02: This plan bears the signature of the institution warden and is approved by the [Agency Authority] at the Central Office level. All major revisions to the plan will be approved by Central Office.

100-01.03: Institution employees are required to become thoroughly familiar with the institution's disturbance control plan and its contents and are to review them annually.

100-01.04: Adequate copies of the plan are available in the Office of the Warden, Office of the Deputy Warden Programs, the mayor's office, and the Training Department for employees to review.

100-02: GUIDELINES FOR DEVELOPMENT OF A DISTURBANCE CONTROL PLAN: As each facility under the supervision of the Department is not totally identical to another, each disturbance is not identical. A detailed uniform procedure for all facilities cannot be written. Therefore, the following plan will serve as a guide. When revisions in the currently approved disturbance control plans are necessary, copies of any changes to any existing plan will be sent to the office of the security administrator at Central Office and to the regional director, for approval prior to inclusion with an existing plan.

100-03: DISTURBANCE TYPES:

100-03.01: Major Disturbance: A disturbance of a riotous nature evidenced by a total lack of control or containment of one or more inmate groups.

100-03.02: General Disturbance: A disturbance with the general intent of accomplishing correction of some real or fancied grievance, or other objective such as an escape. This category would also include passive resistance affecting institutional operations in the form of inmate sit-downs or employee work stoppage.

100-03.03: Minor Disturbance: A disturbance of an isolated nature, such as a fight, or an operational disturbance, such as power outage, water line break, etc., which could produce a momentum to grow to a more serious level.

100-04: REPORTING DISTURBANCES: The
Department of Corrections shall be notified of any disturbances, escapes, violations, or possible violations of law in any institution. Notification shall be made pursuant to [Statute] and follow the chain of command as established in Administrative Policy [Number]. Notification should consist of all essential facts and any new information as the situation develops.

A. Regular Administrative Hours: In the event of a disturbance the Official In Charge shall notify [Name and Telephone Number].

B. Nonregular Administrative Hours: In the event of a disturbance during nonregular hours, the institution duty officer shall notify the Central Office duty officer in accordance with the Central Office Duty Officer Policy/Schedule.

100-05: RESPONSIBILITIES OF CENTRAL
OFFICE PERSONNEL: It is the responsibility of Central Office personnel receiving notification of a disturbance at an institution to collect all essential facts regarding the situation to determine if assistance is required or requested by the institution warden and to relay the information to the director of the Department of Corrections as determined necessary by the nature of the reported disturbance. In all cases, a summary report should be issued and distributed to key departmental personnel.

100-06: REQUESTS FOR ASSISTANCE:
According to the individual nature and requirements of a disturbance, assistance may be determined necessary. Assistance may be requested from various areas in the following manner.

100-06.01: Interdepartmental: Assistance that may be provided to one facility from another facility. This may include equipment or manpower, such as disturbance control teams. Requests for assistance of this nature should be communicated by the institution warden to the regional director.

100-06.02: State Highway Patrol: Calls for assistance by the institution warden may be made on a direct basis to the local patrol post on matters of a minor or routine nature.

[Telephone Number]

The Central Office should be notified of any such request pursuant to Administrative Rule [Reference].

Calls for assistance from the State Highway Patrol where local post resources are inadequate shall be made through the Office of the Director or his designee. These requests will be relayed to the State Highway Patrol Office of Operations [Telephone Number].

Assistance will not be requested of the State Highway Patrol to settle a labor dispute.

100-06.03: [State] National Guard: Calls for assistance by the National Guard must be made to the Office of the Regional Director, and cleared by the director of the Department of Corrections. A call should be made to the National Guard Operations Office to determine if the assistance required is available. If it is determined that the assistance required is available, the director or designee will notify the Governor's Office of the resource need. The Governor's Office, upon notification and approval, will then notify the adjutant general to provide the required assistance.

For this region, the adjutant general will be the National Guard liaison with the institution. [Telephone Number]

100-07: ASSIGNMENT OF CENTRAL OFFICE
PERSONNEL: Based on the nature of the disturbance, the director of the Department of Corrections may elect to provide guidance, advice, or assistance to the institution warden through a third party. This representative shall become the contact or liaison between the institution warden and the director of the Department. The director of the Department may also direct Central Office staff to the institution to provide support services as required in case of an emergency situation.

100-08: NOTIFICATION OF OFF-DUTY
PERSONNEL: A list of all employees, with addresses and telephone numbers, will be maintained. As soon as an emergency is declared, at least one employee will be assigned to contact

the number of off-duty employees necessary to handle the emergency.

Listings are available through the Personnel Office and [Other Locations].

100-09: INSTITUTION DISTURBANCE CONTROL PLAN ELEMENTS: Each institution disturbance control plan shall include at a minimum the following list of elements:

100-09.01: Table of Contents (see pages # and #).

100-09.02: Table of Institution of Organization.

[Typical Organizational Table]

Deputy Warden Responsibilities:

Deputy Warden Operations: Business Office; Cashier; Maintenance; Storeroom; Food Service; Garage.

Deputy Warden Programs: Unit Management Teams; 1st, 2nd, 3rd, and Special Duty Custody Shifts; Key Control; Identification Department; Psychological Service; Social Services; Religious Services; Mail/Visiting Department; Recreation.

Deputy Warden T.I.E. (Training, Industries, and Education): Education; Industries; Job Coordinator.

100-09.03: Identification of Person in Charge.

The warden of the [Name] Correctional Institution or designee will be in charge during any type of emergency or disturbance that may occur at the institution.

In accordance with Administrative Policy [Reference], requiring that the warden designate persons to act in his or her behalf in the event of his or her absence, the deputy warden is to be automatically regarded as the acting warden, unless otherwise directed or instructed by the warden, the director of the Department of Corrections, or the director's designee.

100-09.04: Chain of Command: Presented below is the current chain of command for the [Name] Correctional Institution that will be followed for emergency and non-routine problems. The chain of command is consistent with the institution's other emergency plans and does not necessarily reflect rank and not in all cases does it reflect relative job status.

[List or Show Chart]

When the above-listed personnel are off location, the senior shift officer will assume command. The senior shift officer will initiate immediate efforts to establish communications with the above personnel.

In addition to the listed administrative staff, the following institutions will also be notified:

[List Institutions and Telephone Numbers]

The Tactical Response Teams (TRT) may, at the discretion of the warden or his or her designee, be activated. If it is necessary to activate the TRT teams, the following two persons will be notified to activate the team members:

[List Telephone Numbers]

100-09.05: Notification Procedures, Staff, Agency, and Telephone Numbers.

A. CENTRAL OFFICE PERSONNEL:

[List Telephone Numbers]

If none of the above personnel are available, then contact:

[List Telephone Numbers]

B. EXTERNAL AGENCIES:

[List Telephone Numbers of Local, State, and County Agencies]

100-09.06: Assembly Area Designation: If external forces are required for riot control, they will use the locations listed below as points for assembly:

A. Off-Duty Correctional Staff: Officers Assembly Room, Administration Building.

B. External Agencies: Assembly point will be [Location].

All external agency commanders should report to the Administration Building, where the command post will be located in the Warden's Office.

100-09.07: Command Post Designation: The Office of the Warden is designated as the command post for any type of disturbance that might occur at the institution. In the event the command post cannot be occupied, an auxiliary command post will be established in [Location].

100-09.08: Deployment or Assistance Plan of Responsibilities: The following external forces will be deployed to provide assistance, as necessary.

A. The State Highway Patrol: Will supply adequate forces inside the institution to maintain control. The patrol will also provide helicopter support, as necessary, depending on prevailing weather conditions.

B. The County A Sheriff's Department: Will deploy personnel and provide assistance outside the institution, as necessary.

C. The County B Sheriff's Department: Will provide assistance and support, as available and requested.

D. The City A Police Department: Will provide assistance and support as necessary and requested.

E. The City B Police Department: Will provide helicopter support as necessary or requested depending on prevailing weather conditions.

F. The City C Police Department: Will provide assistance and support as necessary and requested.

G. The National Guard: Will supply adequate forces inside the institution, as necessary, and support for the State Highway Patrol and the facility staff. They will provide any necessary equipment such as emergency lighting, gas masks, tear gas, weapons, food, etc., as necessary and requested.

100-09.09: Press Assembly Area Designation and Policy: News media will be escorted to the [Location]. Telephone service will be made available through the [Location]. The following media will be contacted in the event of a disturbance at the institution:

[List Print, Television, and Radio Contacts, with Telephone Numbers]

In the event of an emergency or other serious condition, public information, news releases, or other dissemination of information will be done only through, and with the approval of, the warden or designee.

In the event an information officer is deemed necessary, [Name and Title] will assume this role.

100-09.10: Provisions for an Incident Log: A chronological log of all events will be maintained whenever any emergency or non-routine problem occurs.

In the event there is an emergency and a recorder is necessary, [Name and Title] will assume this role.

100-09.11: Appointment of Photographer: Under certain circumstances, it is desirable to photograph or videotape the relevant occurrences to provide evidence, documentation, or an element of control and deterrence. The following personnel are familiar with the institution photographic equipment and will act in the order shown as the photographer if necessary:

[Names and Titles]

100-09.12: Hostage Policy: The Hostage Policy is contained in Warden's Security Order

[Reference]. The following information on a hostage's authority and the institution's objective in a hostage incident are provided in this section.

A. HOSTAGES:
   1. In any case where any supervisor and/or employees of the institution are being held hostage by inmates in order to bargain for escape or some other advantage, such officials WILL NOT be considered to be in authority.

   2. NO ORDER given by an official under such circumstances will be obeyed.

B. OBJECTIVES:
   1. Primary:
      a. Ensure the hostages' safety
      b. Apprehend the hostage takers

   2. Secondary:
      a. Minimize casualties on both sides
      b. Neutralize the situation as fast as possible
      c. Provide documentation of the situation

100-09.13: Maps of the institution with the alert posts, fire hydrants, and helipads. The following maps are included in Appendix #1:

A. Plot Plan, [Name] Correctional Institution

B. Institution map showing alert posts and helipad

C. Institution map showing fire hydrant locations

100-09.14: Designation of Key Hot Spots: The institution has identified several key hot spots. At the onset of a disturbance, additional security may be needed at any one of the locations to secure and control these areas. Floor plans of all buildings are included in Appendix #2.

O.C.I. Key Hot Spots are:

[List]

100-09.15: Arsenal Equipment List. The following equipment is available in the arsenal and other designated areas on the grounds.

A. WEAPONS: QUANTITY
[List type and quantity]

   CN Gas Grenades:

   [List type and quantity]

   CN Projectiles:

   [List type and quantity]

   Smoke Grenades:

   [List type and quantity]

B. RIOT EQUIPMENT:

[List type and quantity]

C. AMMUNITION:

[List type and quantity]

D. RESTRAINING EQUIPMENT:

[List type and quantity]

100-09.16: Communications Equipment List and Available Frequencies.

The [Name] Correctional Institution has the following communications equipment capability:

[List type and quantity]

The Call Sign for all radio units is [Sign].

Frequencies:

[List]

100-10: TYPICAL CONTRIBUTING FACTORS TO A DISTURBANCE:

100-10.01: Racial or gang problems.

100-10.02: Complaints concerning the quantity and/or quality of food served.

100-10.03: Dissatisfaction with the performance or attitude of an employee assigned to a certain post.

100-10.04: Medical complaints regarding treatment or type of treatment.

100-10.05: Complaints concerning visits, recreation, mail, or commissary privileges.

100-10.06: Misinformation relayed to inmates.

100-10.07: High incidence of assaults.

100-10.08: Outside influences.

100-10.09: Parole Board complaints.

100-10.10: Inmate work assignment complaints.

100-11: SIGNS OF TENSION:

100-11.01: A general atmosphere of sullenness, restlessness, or irascibleness among the inmate population.

100-11.02: General staff avoidance by the inmate population.

100-11.03: Large number of cell, dorm, or job change requests.

100-11.04: Large number of institutional transfer requests.

100-11.05: Meal avoidance.

100-11.06: A general lack of communication by inmates to staff.

100-11.07: An unusual increase in commissary purchases.

100-11.08: Increase in self-segregation by racial or ethnic groups or unusual inmate gatherings.

100-12: PREVENTATIVE ACTION: Quick, decisive action by officers and supervisory staff will often prevent the spread of any disturbance. In addition, any of the following may tend to prevent riots:

100-12.01: Good communication concerning plans, programs, or procedures.

100-12.02: Reduction of misunderstandings between inmates.

100-12.03: Constructive work and recreational programs for inmates.

100-12.04: Prompt reporting methods designed to keep supervisors informed about trouble spots, gang information, and group disagreements.

100-12.05: A good inmate personnel, security, and classification system that identifies potential leaders and monitors their activity.

100-12.06: Fair and impartial treatment of inmates.

100-12.07: An understanding relationship between staff and inmates.

100-13: ORDER OF RESPONSIBILITY: In considering a course of action, responsibilities should be considered in the following order:

100-13.01: General public safety.

100-13.02: Safety and welfare of hostages.

100-13.03: Prevention of loss of life or injury to other staff.

100-13.04: Inmate welfare.

100-13.05: Protection of property.

100-14: STEPS TO BE TAKEN: In the event a riot does occur, it will usually begin suddenly, spread rapidly, and cause heavy damage. It is necessary to promptly activate the disturbance plan, considering the following steps:

100-14.01: Containment of the rioters.

100-14.02: Immediate steps to close any avenues of escape are mandatory. The trouble should be localized and access to other areas cut off to prevent the disorder from spreading. This includes securing the perimeter.

100-14.03: An estimate of the situation should be made before rushing in or committing officers to a situation that might result in their being taken hostage. If necessary, reinforcements should be called and the required equipment to handle the trouble assembled. This period of delay can be used to plan the operation and determine the immediate objective.

Upon being called, or otherwise alerted, all off-duty personnel will report to the institution in regular duty attire as expeditiously as possible. Members of special units will wear the appropriate attire for their units. They will report to the Officer's Assembly Room for assignment.

100-14.04: The safety of employees and inmates must be considered if the use of force or defensive equipment becomes necessary. Such force or equipment shall be used only when ordered by the warden or his or her representative in charge.

100-14.05: ANY PERSON HELD AS HOSTAGE HAS NO AUTHORITY, REGARDLESS OF RANK, WHILE UNDER DURESS.

100-14.06: A general order of dispersal should be made over the public address system, bullhorn, or other means of mass communication.

Personnel at the scene of the disturbance will try to stop the disorder when it first occurs by verbal orders, threats of force, or force, if it is prudent to try. If this is not possible, they should:

A. Attempt to secure the area by locking doors or other appropriate actions.

B. Safeguard tools, keys, and other materials that could be used by the rioters.

C. After making a reasonable attempt to quell the disorder and secure the area, if in personal danger, retreat from the area.

D. If retreat is not possible, attempt to isolate yourself by locking yourself in a cell or other secure area.

E. If retreat is not possible, dispose of keys by throwing them out of a window, flushing them down a commode, or any other method that would ensure that the keys do not get into the rioters' hands.

No person at the scene of a disturbance will negligently flee his/her duty post; however, personnel are expected to make reasonable efforts to avoid being taken hostage.

100-14.07: Nonparticipants: The opportunity will be given for all inmates not wishing to participate in the disturbance to withdraw from the disturbed area. They should be provided safe conduct to a secure area of the facility.

100-14.08: Cause: The cause of the disturbance will be ascertained, if possible.

Attempts to confer with rioters will be made and they should be urged to select a spokesman to confer with the institution warden or his or her representative.

No promises should be made regarding any of the demands presented other than that they will receive a fair hearing.

100-14.09: Leaders: Employees should be instructed to closely observe the inmate rioters' actions to provide evidence later as to the agitators and ringleaders involved.

100-14.10: Log: A senior staff member will be immediately assigned to keep an ongoing log of events of the disturbance, noting persons involved, times, etc.

100-15: SUBJUGATION OF RIOTERS: When the decision to use force to control the disturbance has been made, the kind and amount of force to be used will be dictated by the situation.

100-15.01: Riot Squads: All officers will be properly equipped with the necessary protective equipment.

Each squad will be given specific instructions as to the course of action. Squads should enter the disturbed areas simultaneously from as many entrances as are available.

Only the force necessary to control the situation will be used, but this statement in and of itself is not enough in any report of use of force. The report should be very specific as to the kind of provocation or threatening acts taken by the inmate, with very specific language regarding the specific action taken by staff to control the situation.

100-15.02: Water: It is possible to bring a riotous situation under control by the effective use of water.

Location of hydrants, availability of hose and other fire-fighting equipment will be part of the disturbance plan. Further, hydrants, valves, and exposed pipes should be assigned to specific zones for protection during demonstrations.

Water may be used to disperse participants of a riot, to bring sporadic fires under control before they become extensive, and to create dampness necessary to the most effective concentration of gas, should the occasion develop.

100-15.03: Gas: Should there be a larger number of rioters so situated that their removal would be hazardous to either inmates or personnel, the decision to use gas may be made. This decision must be made by the warden or the person in charge of the facility.

CS gas should be used only in open outside areas. It should not be used at any time inside any building or structure of the facility.

100-15.04: Firearms: Personnel will be authorized to use firearms only as a last resort to prevent escapes, protect state property, and to prevent injury or loss of life of personnel or inmates who are held hostage.

Whenever possible, orders to halt or to desist will first be given. Whenever firearms are used, only that force necessary to stop the offensive action shall be employed.

Weapons shall be issued only to people who are proficient in the use of the weapon to be issued.

100-15.05: Cameras: Pictorial documentation of disturbance conditions, including situations where physical confrontation is possible, scenes of specific areas before entry by emergency or assistance units, should be used. Staff members who are familiar with and trained in the use of both photographic and video equipment will be assigned to fulfill this requirement.

100-16: POST RIOT: The following steps will be taken as soon as the disturbance is under control to ensure that no one has escaped and that the physical plan of the facility is secure:

100-16.01: Confinement of all participants of the disturbance and assignment of sufficient supervision to prevent a reoccurrence.

100-16.02: An accounting of all inmates.

100-16.03: Sufficient supervision assigned to all housing units and the dining area until it is ascertained that the disturbance is completely subdued.

100-16.04: Segregation of all leaders and agitators.

100-16.05: If necessary, the curtailment of all work and recreation activities and the rescheduling of dining hall use so that it is possible to provide supervision over small groups of inmates during meal periods. Whenever possible, participants should be fed in their cell areas.

100-16.06: An extensive and thorough investigation by interviewing ringleaders and active participants should be commenced.

100-16.07: Employees and outside agency participants involved in or witnessing the disturbance should be interviewed and statements taken accordingly.

100-16.08: Immediate arrangements for repair of damage to the physical facility will be made.

100-16.09: All damaged areas and destruction will be photographed before repairs are made.

100-16.10: Provisions for securing inmates' personal property and labeling of property are to be completed.

100-16.11: Immediate medical attention for all reported injuries.

100-17: LENGTH OF EFFECTIVENESS: The foregoing orders supersede all existing orders relative to Disturbance Control Procedures for the [Name] Correctional Institution and will remain in effect until revised or rescinded in writing by the offices of the undersigned.

100-18: APPENDICES:

APPENDIX: SUBJECT

1. Maps of institution, hydrants, etc.

2. Building Plans

3. Posts that can be vacated in an emergency

[Signature]
Warden

[Co-signature]
[Designated Central Office official]

APPENDIX F

Guidelines for Hostages

■ Be cautious of heroics. Don't act foolishly.

■ Be cooperative and obey hostage takers' demands without appearing either servile or antagonistic.

■ Look for a protected place where you could dive or roll if either authorities or inmates attempt to assault your location with force.

■ Keep your cool. Attempt to relax by thinking about pleasant scenes or memories. You might try to recollect the plots of books or movies. This will help you remain functional.

■ Keep a low profile. Avoid the appearance of observing crimes that rioters commit. Look down or away. Avoid interfering with their discussions or activities.

■ Do not make threats against hostage takers or give any indication that you would testify against them. If inmates are attempting to conceal their identities, make no indication that you recognize them.

■ Be reluctant to give up your identification or clothes. Loss of these things is demoralizing. Inmates will use them for bargaining. Be especially resistant to exchange clothes with an inmate. This could put you in much greater danger in case of an assault.

■ As a result of the stress of the hostage situation, you may have difficulty retaining fluids. Try to drink water and eat even if you are not hungry. It is important to maintain strength.

■ Be conscious of your body language as well as your speech. Do not say or do anything to arouse the hostility or suspicions of your captors. Act neutral and be a good listener if your captors want to talk. Be cautious about making suggestions to your captors—you may be held responsible if something you suggest goes wrong.

■ Think of persuasive reasons the hostage takers should keep you and the other hostages alive and not harm you. Encourage them to let authorities know of your whereabouts and condition. Suggest possible ways where you or others may benefit your captors in negotiations that would free you.

■ If you as a hostage end up serving as negotiator between inmates and authorities, messages between the two groups should be conveyed accurately.

■ If there is an assault to rescue and shots are fired, drop quickly to the floor and seek cover. Keep your hands on your head. When appropriate, identify yourself. Do not resist being apprehended until positive identification is made.

■ There is a tremendous psychological and physiological relief when you are released. You should be debriefed. This will give you the opportunity to discuss what happened to you and how you feel. Express your feelings freely. Deal openly with your reactions and any problems you may have subsequently. You have nothing to be ashamed of.

■ Even though you must appear disinterested while being held hostage, observe all you can. Ensure that you are thoroughly debriefed and make your own notes after your release. All of these things will help in the subsequent prosecution of the rioters.

References

Alper, B. S. *Prison inside-out.* 1974. Cambridge, Mass.: Ballinger Publishing Co.

American Correctional Association. 1979. *Legal responsibility and authority of correctional officers.* College Park, Md.: American Correctional Association.

American Correctional Association. 1987. *Guidelines for the development of a security program.* Laurel, Md.: American Correctional Association.

Arnold, J., et al. 1980. *Holocaust at New Mexico State Penitentiary.* Lubbock, Tex.: C. F. Boone.

Balton, M. "Hostage negotiations: alternative to SWAT." *Law enforcement news.* December 1975-January 1976: 1-2.

Bolz, F., and Hersey, E. 1979. *Hostage cop.* New York: Rawson, Wade.

Cawley, D. F. "Anatomy of a siege." *The police chief.* January 1974: 30-34.

Desroches, F. "The April 1971 Kingston Penitentiary riot." *Canadian journal of criminology and corrections.* 16(4): 332-351.

DiIulio, J. J., Jr. 1987. *Governing prisons.* New York: The Free Press, Macmillan, Inc.

Edwards, R. V. 1977. *Crisis intervention and how it works.* Springfield, Ill.: Charles C Thomas.

Federal Laboratories. *Chemical weapons training manual.* Saltsburg, Pa.: Federal Laboratories.

Fox, V. "Prison riots in a democratic society." *Police.* August 1972: 33-41.

Fox, V. "Why prisoners riot." *Federal probation.* 35(1): 9-14.

Garson, G. "Force versus restraint in prison riots." *Crime and delinquency.* 18(4): 411-421.

Gettinger, S. April 1980. "Informer, rat, snitch, fink, stool pigeon, squealer." *Corrections magazine.* 6(2): 17-19.

Illinois Legislative Investigative Commission. *The Joliet Correctional Center Riot of April 22, 1975.* (Report to the Illinois General Assembly)

Jenkins, B., et al. 1977. *Numbered lives: some statistical observations from 77 international hostage episodes.* Santa Monica, Calif.: Rand Corporation.

Johnson, P. 1989. *Understanding prisons: a correctional manual.* Jackson, Mich.: Correctional Consultants, Inc.

Johnson, R. 1977. "Ameliorating prison stress: some helping roles for custodial personnel." *International journal of criminology and penology,* pp. 263-273.

Kahn, B., and Zinn, N. January 1979. "Prison gangs in the community." *Journal of California law enforcement.* 13(3).

Koga, R. K. 1967. *The Koga method: police weaponless control and defensive tactics.* Los Angeles, Calif.

Momboisse, R. M., and Thomas, C. C. 1977. *Riots, revolts and insurrections.* Springfield, Ill.: Charles C Thomas.

National Institute of Corrections. 1985. *Managing long term inmates.* Washington, D.C.

Needham, J. P. 1977. *Neutralization of prison hostage situations.* Criminal Justice Monograph 8, No. 1. Huntsville, Tex.: Sam Houston State University.

Office of the Attorney General, State of New Mexico. 1980. *Report of the attorney general on the February 2 and 3, 1980 riot at the penitentiary of New Mexico.* Santa Fe, N.M.: Office of the Attorney General.

The Official Report of the New York Commission on Attica. 1972. *Attica.* New York: Bantam Books.

Potter, J. April 1980. "Annual population survey: growth slows at least for now." *Corrections magazine.* 6(2): 25-30.

"Prisoners in 1988." April 1989. *Bureau of Justice Statistics bulletin.* U.S. Department of Justice: Washington, D.C.

Smith, A. 1973. "The conflict theory of riots," in *Collective violence in correctional institutions: a search for causes.* South Carolina Department of Corrections Collective Violence Research Project. Columbia, S.C.: State Printing Co.

Toch, H. 1978. "Social climate and prison violence," *Federal probation* 42(4): 21-25.

U.S. Bureau of Prisons. 1988. "A report to the attorney general on the Cuban detainee uprisings." Washington, D.C.

U.S. Department of Justice. Law Enforcement Assistance Administration. National Institute of Law Enforcement and Criminal Justice. 1976. *Controlled confrontation.* Washington, D.C.: U.S. Government Printing Office.

U.S. House of Representatives. Internal Security Committee. 1973. *Revolutionary target: the American penal system.* Washington, D.C.: U.S. Government Printing Office.

Willis, H. L., Sr. *Defensive tactics, basic consideration.* Petersburg, Va.: Virginia Union College.

Wolk, R., and Umina, A. *The selection of crisis intervention specialists* (unpublished paper).

Selected Publications Available Through ACA

Classification as a Management Tool: Theories and Models for Decision-Makers

Constitutional Rights of Prisoners

Correctional Career Logbook

Correctional Officer Resource Guide, 2nd edition

Correctional Officers: Correctional Issues

Correctional Officers: Power, Pressure and Responsibility

Corrections in America, 5th edition

Corrections Today

Correspondence Courses

Corrections in America: An Introduction

Counseling the Involuntary and Resistant Client

Curbing the Abuses of Inmate Litigation

Current International Trends in Corrections

Design Guide for Secure Adult Correctional Facilities

Elements of Short-term Group Counseling revision

From Cell to Society

Games Criminals Play and How You Can Profit by Knowing Them

Issues in Correctional Training and Casework, Volume 4

Issues in Juvenile Delinquency

Jails in America: An Overview of Issues

Legal Responsibility and Authority of Correctional Officers

Literacy: A Concept for All Seasons (An Offender Programs Handbook)

Litigation and You

Managing Adult Inmates: Classification for Housing and Program Assignment

National Jail & Adult Detention Directory of Juvenile & Adult Correctional Institutions & Agencies

Nurturing Today: Families of Prisoners

Offender Assessment and Evaluation

Older Offenders: Perspectives in Criminology and Criminal Justice

Politics of a Prison Riot

Potential Liabilities of Probation and Parole Officers

Prison Personnel Management and Staff Development

Prison Violence in America

Prisons and Kids

Probation & Parole, Electronic Surveillance: Correctional Issues

Protective Custody in Adult Correctional Facilities

The State of Corrections, Proceedings

Stress Management for Correctional Officers and Their Families

An Uncommon Task and Other Stories

Vital Statistics in Corrections

Women and Criminality; The Woman as Victim, Offender, and Practitioner

For ordering information, contact the American Correctional Association, 8025 Laurel Lakes Court, Laurel, MD 20707, (301) 206-5100.

Notes